JOSEPH

A Man of Integrity & Forgiveness

BIBLE STUDY GUIDE

From the Bible-teaching ministry of

CHARLES R. SWINDOLL

INSIGHT FOR LIVING

Chuck graduated in 1963 from Dallas Theological Seminary, where he now serves as the school's fourth president, helping to prepare a new generation of men and women for the ministry. Chuck has served in pastorates in three states: Massachusetts, Texas, and California, including almost twenty-three years at the First Evangelical Free Church in Fullerton, California. His sermon messages have been aired over radio since 1979 as the *Insight for Living* broadcast. A best-selling author, Chuck has written numerous books and booklets on many subjects.

Based on the outlines and transcripts of Chuck's sermons, the study guide text is co-authored by Lee Hough, a graduate of the University of Texas at Arlington and Dallas Theological Seminary. He also wrote the Living Insights and Questions for Group Discussion.

Editor in Chief:
Cynthia Swindoll

Coauthor:
Lee Hough

Senior Editor and Assistant Writer:
Wendy Peterson

Copy Editors:
Deborah Gibbs
Marco Salazar
Glenda Schlahta

Text Designer:
Gary Lett

Graphics System Administrator:
Bob Haskins

Director, Communications Division:
John Norton

Production Coordinator:
Don Bernstein

Project Coordinator:
Shannon Scharkey

Unless otherwise identified, all Scripture references are from the New American Standard Bible, updated edition, copyright © The Lockman Foundation 1960, 1962, 1963, 1968, 1971, 1972, 1973, 1975, 1977, 1995. Used by permission.
The other translation cited is the *King James Version* [KJV].

ISBN 1-57972-075-7

STUDY GUIDE COVER DESIGN: Ron Lara. Adapted from the hardback cover design by D² Design Works; hardback illustration by Jeff Barson.
Printed in the United States of America

CONTENTS

INTRODUCTION

Incarnate the truth!"

I can still hear one of my favorite seminary profs saying that. I have repeated it on numerous occasions myself. It is a helpful and accurate statement. Abstract truth seems sterile and difficult to grasp when it stands alone—but when we see it illustrated in a life as that life models such truth, it's amazing how clearly it emerges and how attainable it becomes. This, of course, is the genius behind any biography.

Joseph is a classic example. He embodies some of the most significant truths in all of Scripture. Although a man just like us, Joseph blazes a new trail through a jungle of mistreatment, loneliness, false accusations, *undeserved* punishment, and gross misunderstanding. He exemplifies forgiveness, freedom from bitterness, and an unbelievably positive attitude toward those who had done him harm. From one episode to the next, you will literally shake you head in amazement.

That's the way it is when mere humanity incarnates divine truth. My prayer is that this principle will not stop with Joseph.

Chuck Swindoll

Chuck Swindoll

Broadcast Schedule

Joseph: A Man of Integrity and Forgiveness

June 23–July 24, 1998

Tuesday	June 23	**Favored Son, Hated Brother** *Genesis 37*
Wednesday	June 24	**Favored Son, Hated Brother**
Thursday	June 25	**Resisting Temptation** *Genesis 39*
Friday	June 26	**Resisting Temptation**
Monday	June 29	**Imprisoned and Forgotten** *Genesis 39:20–41:1*
Tuesday	June 30	**Imprisoned and Forgotten**
Wednesday	July 1	**Remembered and Promoted** *Genesis 41:1–46*
Thursday	July 2	**Remembered and Promoted**
Friday	July 3	**Reaping the Rewards of Righteousness** *Genesis 41:41–47*
Monday	July 6	**Reaping the Rewards of Righteousness**
Tuesday	July 7	**Activating a Seared Conscience** *Genesis 42:1–28*
Wednesday	July 8	**Activating a Seared Conscience**
Thursday	July 9	**Groanings of a Sad Dad** *Genesis 42:29–43:15*
Friday	July 10	Groanings of a Sad Dad
Monday	July 13	**Fear Displaced by Grace** *Genesis 43:15–34*
Tuesday	July 14	**Fear Displaced by Grace**
Wednesday	July 15	**"I Am Joseph!"** *Genesis 44:1–45:15*
Thursday	July 16	**"I Am Joseph!"**
Friday	July 17	**The Ultimate Family Reunion** *Genesis 45:16–46:7, 28–30*

Monday	July 20	**The Ultimate Family Reunion**
Tuesday	July 21	**On-the-Job Integrity** *Genesis 46:31–47:26*
Wednesday	July 22	**On-the-Job Integrity**
Thursday	July 23	**Highlights of Twilight and Midnight** *Genesis 47:29–31; 50:15–21*
Friday	July 24	**Highlights of Twilight and Midnight**

Insight for Living • Post Office Box 69000, Anaheim, CA 92817-0900
Insight for Living Ministries • Post Office Box 2510, Vancouver, BC, Canada V6B 3W7
Insight for Living, Inc. • GPO Box 2823 EE, Melbourne, VIC 3001, Australia

Printed in the United States of America

PUTTING TRUTH
INTO ACTION

K nowledge apart from application falls short of God's desire for
His children. He wants us to apply what we learn so that we
will change and grow. This study guide was prepared with these
goals in mind. As you go through the following pages, we hope your
desire to discover biblical truth will grow as your understanding of
God's Word increases and that you will be encouraged to apply what
you've learned.

To assist you in your study, we've included a section called
Living Insights at the end of each lesson. These exercises will
challenge you to study further and to think of specific ways to put
your discoveries into action.

In this edition, we've added **Questions for Group Discussion,**
which are formulated to get your group talking about the key issues
in each lesson.

There are many ways to use this guide—in personal devotions,
group studies, discussions with friends and family, and Sunday school
classes. And, of course, it's an ideal study aid when you're listening
to its corresponding *Insight for Living* radio series.

To benefit most from this study guide, we would encourage you
to consider it a spiritual journal. That's why we've included space
in the **Living Insights** for recording your thoughts and discoveries.
We hope you'll return to those sections often for review and encouragement as you continue to grow in your walk with Christ.

Lee Hough
Coauthor of Text
Author of Living Insights and
Questions for Group Discussion

JOSEPH

A Man of Integrity & Forgiveness

Chapter 1

FAVORED SON, HATED BROTHER
Genesis 37

Reading the Bible is sometimes like sitting on one of those wide front porches your grandparents used to have—the kind where you had a porch-swing view of the whole neighborhood. Only from the Bible's inspired veranda, your view stretches from an earth under construction at one end of the block all the way to the shiny streets of a new heaven and earth at the other.

Quite a view. And there are lots of neighbors too. If you look off in the direction of Genesis, you can see Adam working up a sweat, or Noah stocking a boat, or two old timers—Abraham and Sarah—out promenading their little baby, Isaac. A couple of books up from those folks live David and his best friend Jonathan. Just a stone's throw from them lives an important fellow named Nehemiah, who is cupbearer to King Artaxerxes. And next door to him is Esther; she's being raised by her cousin Mordecai.

You'd probably be surprised at how many Christians have never taken the time to come down from the New Testament side of the street to meet some of their Old Testament neighbors. That's what we want to do in this study—take you down the block to the first book in the Bible and introduce you to an unforgettable fellow. Someone whose biography occupies more space in Genesis than Adam, Noah, Abraham, or even his own father, Jacob. Someone who responded to broken dreams and impossible circumstances with a faith that propelled him from the pit of slavery to the pinnacle of power.

That fellow, whose doorstep we'll be camping on, is Joseph. He had quite an unusual life. One that the apostle Paul guaranteed would instruct us on how to live, offer us encouragement, and

1

provide us with warnings and timely reproofs (compare Rom. 15:4; 1 Cor. 10:11; 2 Tim. 3:16–17).

If you're ready, let's walk down the street and meet this young man who was the favorite of his father but the hated brother of his siblings.

A Brief Overview

Before we are formally introduced to Joseph, let's gather some brief background information, looking specifically at three distinct segments of his biography.

Birth to age seventeen (Gen. 30:24–37:2). If Joseph's life were a storm, this period would be the clouds swelling up to eclipse the sun. The family was in transition, unsettled, moving. A growing sense of agitation was in the wind. You could hear the low rumblings of pain and discontent building as his family clashed in jealousy, lust, and hatred.

Seventeen to age thirty (37:2–41:46). As Joseph entered into young manhood, the brewing storm finally burst, triggered by his brothers' rejection of him. Enslavement and imprisonment rained down on him.

Thirty to death (41:46–50:26). The last eighty years of his life were years of prosperity under God's blessing. Joseph had a perfect opportunity to exact revenge on his brothers, to blot out the sun from their lives, but he blessed and brightened their lives instead.

Setting the Stage

Now that we have a feel for the overall direction of Joseph's life, let's go back to the beginning and see how it all started.

The home in which Joseph grew up was anything but a place of shelter. It was, instead, the eye of a storm. And the front door that lets us in to this turbulent biography is found in Genesis 37.

This chapter introduces us to the middle section of Joseph's life and works forward from there. The first person we encounter—and need to understand—is Joseph's father, Jacob. His other name is Israel, meaning "God strives," and it was given to him after he wrestled with God and clung to Him for a blessing (see 32:22–32). This name was a tremendous improvement over his original name, which meant "chiseler" or "deceiver."

Jacob: The Aging Father

From his earliest years Jacob had a knack for living up to his original name (see Gen. 27). He cheated and lied his way along and, except for a few brief interludes of piety, couldn't be trusted.

Jacob's marriages also plagued his family with instability. He had two wives who were also sisters, Leah and Rachel, but Rachel was the one he loved (Gen. 29). This set up a rivalry that resulted in a childbearing competition.

Leah was the first to have children, and she eventually produced seven: six boys and a girl named Dinah. Rachel, however, was barren—a disgrace for a woman in those times. So she had her handmaiden, Bilhah, sleep with Jacob so that she might have children through her. Bilhah eventually bore Jacob two sons. Not to be outdone, Leah retaliated by having her handmaiden, Zilpah, lay with Jacob, and she bore him two sons also (Gen. 29–30). Finally, Rachel herself bore a child, and she named him Joseph[1] (30:22–24).

Add all this up and you've got one husband, two wives, two concubines, four mothers, eleven sons, and one daughter—which did not equal marital bliss. Instead, there were jealousy, strife, anger, lust, deceit, competition, and secrecy.

By this time Jacob was no longer a young man. He'd worked in Haran for his father-in-law, Laban, a total of twenty years. During that time, there had been a lot of family infighting and deception on the part of both father-in-law and son-in-law. So Jacob decided to move his family back to Canaan, his homeland (v. 25).

Canaan: The Promised Land

The trip home came to an abrupt halt, however, when the family reached the land of the Hivites and the city of Shechem. There the daughter of Jacob and Leah, Dinah, was raped (34:1–2).

Incredibly, when Jacob heard of the despicable act, he did nothing. But her brothers did. They killed not only the man who raped Dinah but also every male in the city . . . regardless of the fact that they had nothing to do with the rape (vv. 3–26). After his sons had looted the town (vv. 27–29), Jacob finally voiced a concern over the situation. But it wasn't about the welfare of his daughter.

---

1. Joseph means "may He add." It was an expression of Rachel's hope that God would give her another son.

He was more concerned about his public image among the surrounding peoples (vv. 30–31).

So the family moved on, but it wasn't long before a second tragedy struck. While en route to the next city, Jacob's beloved Rachel died giving birth to their second child, Joseph's brother Benjamin (35:16–18).

Jacob had worked fourteen years to marry Rachel. They had waited long for Joseph to be born. And now, after another long wait, Benjamin was born, but at the expense of the one woman whom Jacob had truly loved.

After the funeral the family moved on again—right into a third tragic situation: Reuben, the oldest son, committed incest with one of his father's concubines (v. 22a). The text clearly states that Jacob heard about it. But, just as when his daughter was raped, Jacob let things go on as if nothing had happened.[2]

What started out as an exciting trip home ended up being a gauntlet of grief. The final blow came after Jacob reached Canaan, when his father, Isaac, died (35:27–29).

Joseph: The Favorite Son

Jacob's arrival in Canaan brings us back to Genesis 37 and the front door of Joseph's biography. The clouds hanging over Joseph's family at this juncture in his life were like dark bruises, swollen with the pain of years of unresolved conflicts. Yet in the midst of all this, Jacob discovered a refuge, a shelter against the turbulence he felt within the rest of his family.

> Now Israel [Jacob] loved Joseph more than all his sons, because he was the son of his old age. (v. 3a)

Doting on Joseph may have brightened Jacob's world, but it brought only dark clouds into Joseph's. And Joseph's own tattling on his brothers in verse 2 did nothing to dispel those clouds.

Then there was the matter of a certain coat.

The Brothers: Jealous Conflict

> And [Jacob] made [Joseph] a varicolored tunic. His brothers saw that their father loved him more than

---

2. Jacob may have acted as if nothing had happened, but he knew his son had committed a great sin and he never forgot it. Years later, when this passive father lay on his deathbed, he finally did address the evil that had been done (see Gen. 49:1–4).

all his brothers; and so they hated him and could
not speak to him on friendly terms. (vv. 3b–4)

This tunic was more than a simple gift from a loving father. It
was a long-sleeved garment worn by the nobility of the day, a symbol
of authority and favored position within the family.[3] And the rest
of Jacob's sons jealously hated Joseph for it.

That hatred dug in a little deeper when Joseph related a dream
to his brothers in which he became their ruler (vv. 5–8). Then
Joseph told of another dream, this time with Jacob listening, where
again everyone in the family was bowing down to him (vv. 9–11).
Jacob wasn't too fond of Joseph's words, but still he did nothing to
assuage the ill feelings that were driving a wedge between Joseph
and his brothers. He simply "kept the saying in mind" (v. 11) and
ignored the thundering signs of the oncoming storm.

A Plan to Kill Joseph

"When it is evening, you say, 'It will be fair weather,
for the sky is red.' And in the morning, 'There will
be a storm today, for the sky is red and threatening.'
Do you know how to discern the appearance of the
sky, but cannot discern the signs of the times?"
(Matt. 16:2–3)

Jesus was speaking to the Pharisees and Sadducees, but He could
just as well have been speaking to Jacob.

Sent by Father

Like any good shepherd, Jacob knew how to discern the meaning of the sky's appearance. But he chose to ignore the red, threatening signs that hung over his own family. He closed his eyes to
the danger of sending Joseph to check up on his brothers, who were
pasturing the family's flock in Shechem (Gen. 37:12–17).

Mistreated by Brothers

When Joseph finally spotted his brothers with the flock, they
were in Dothan, twenty miles north of Shechem. Twenty miles

---

3. "Jacob presented Joseph with a coat of many colours (KJV), or a coat with long sleeves,
which set him in a class apart and exempted him from the menial tasks of farming." Joyce
G. Baldwin, *The Message of Genesis 12–50: From Abraham to Joseph*, The Bible Speaks Today
Series (Downers Grove, Ill.: InterVarsity Press, 1986), p. 159.

north of the city where those same brothers had slaughtered every male out of rage over their sister's rape.

Seeing Joseph coming, the brothers immediately held a family council (v. 18). The time had come to vent their wrath again, just as they had done in Shechem. The only question to be settled was how.

> "Now then, come and let us kill him and throw him into one of the pits; and we will say, 'A wild beast devoured him.'" (v. 20a)

Reuben, however, interceded on Joseph's behalf and persuaded the others to put him in a pit instead of killing him outright.[4] When Joseph arrived, they stripped him of the coat Jacob had given him, threw him in a pit, and coolly sat down to eat (vv. 21–25a).

A Caravan to Egypt

While they were eating, and while Reuben was gone, the brothers decided to sell Joseph to a passing caravan of Ishmaelites. Next, they poured goat's blood on his tunic, and when they got home they deceived their father into thinking Joseph was killed by a wild animal. Jacob wept bitterly (vv. 25b–35).

In a way, all the things Jacob had been too passive and preoccupied to deal with in the past finally crashed in on him. Behind the cruel and deceitful actions of his sons lay many accusing questions. Where were you, Jacob, when Dinah was raped? When your sons slaughtered the men in Shechem? When Reuben committed incest? When the whole family was being torn apart by jealousy and anger?

As the shepherd of a large family, Jacob had refused to see or do anything about the red sky warnings that had spread over his flock. He had let his children sow the wind, until they reaped a whirlwind (see Hos. 8:7).

Meanwhile, Joseph was taken into Egypt and sold as a slave to the captain of the guard in Pharaoh's court (Gen. 37:36).

Four Lessons to Be Learned

Imagine your own siblings tossing you into a pit to die, then sitting down for dinner. Imagine being sold as a slave, taken to a

---

4. To his credit, Reuben not only saved Joseph's life but secretly planned his rescue (vv. 21–22).

country you didn't know, to be owned by a man you'd never seen. And all this while you were only seventeen years old!

All we can do is imagine. However, we can glean from Joseph's experience four real lessons that can be just as important for us today as they were for Joseph.

First: *No family is exempt from adversity.* There is no place in this fallen world where one can escape trials. There is only One who can give you the refuge and strength to endure and grow through them (see Ps. 46).

Second: *No enemy is more subtle than passivity.* Do you know how passive parents tend to discipline? Usually in anger. For weeks, months, even years, these individuals try to avoid dealing with problems until one day these problems explode. And in a brutal moment they'll come down on someone with both feet. But that isn't discipline. The child they leave behind after one of these scorching sessions will be no more disciplined than before, only angry and alienated. We've got to realize that giving in to the subtle urge to avoid issues now only creates problems in the future.

Third: *No response is more cruel than jealousy.* Solomon was right when he said that jealousy is as cruel as the grave (Song of Sol. 8:6 kjv). If you let the seed of jealousy take root in your children, it will destroy the family's unity and harmony. As a parent, you must learn to recognize and weed out bad attitudes as well as actions. And in addition to your weeding responsibilities, don't forget to water your children with praise when they display the right attitudes.

Fourth: *No condition is more unfair than slavery.* In one day Joseph went from a favored son to a faceless slave, from luxury's pillows to Egypt's bonds. No one in Joseph's family knew where he ended up, not even the brothers who sold him. But God knew where he was. And no amount of unfair circumstances could thwart His plan to raise Joseph from pit to pinnacle.

Living Insights

In his book *How to Really Love Your Child,* Dr. Ross Campbell asserts,

> The husband who will take full, total, overall responsibility for his family, and take the initiative in conveying his love to his wife and children, will

7

experience unbelievable rewards: a loving, apprecia-
tive, helping wife who will be her loveliest for him;
children who are safe, secure, content and able to
grow to be their best. . . . Fathers, the initiative
must be ours.[5]

Jacob did not take the initiative for the overall responsibility
of his family or for conveying his love—except to Rachel, Joseph,
and later Benjamin. And it cost him and his family dearly. Take a
moment to look beneath the surface of this outwardly prosperous
family and paint a verbal picture of the painful emotional consequences they endured because of a passive father.

_____

_____

_____

_____

_____

Dads, are you taking the initiative in conveying to your
children—in ways they can understand—that they are loved? Have
you told them lately that you love them? What are some other
ways, verbally, that your love can be communicated?

_____

_____

_____

_____

What are some of the nonverbal ways you communicate your love?

_____

_____

_____

_____

5. D. Ross Campbell, *How to Really Love Your Child* (Wheaton, Ill.: Scripture Press Publications, Victor Books, 1977), p. 23.

Reflect for a moment on the ways that your father conveyed—or didn't convey—his love for you. Are you repeating any of those verbal and nonverbal patterns?

_____

_____

_____

_____

Last, taking the initiative is essential, but so is pausing to consider whether your attempts at love are being _understood_. What conveyed love to you as a child may mean absolutely nothing to your children. This isn't an issue of right or wrong; rather, it's one of good communication. As parents, we must learn to convey our love in a language that _our_ children understand. Are you confident that your messages of love are being heard? How? If not, what can you do about it?

_____

_____

_____

_____

Questions for Group Discussion

A word to the group leader: The Questions for Group Discussion throughout this guide are meant to assist you, not burden you. What we have provided is a smorgasbord of ideas for you to use in nourishing your group. There's no need to answer all of the questions—feel free to choose the ones that best fit your overall needs. And if some of these questions spark ideas of your own, by all means do not limit yourself to what is written here. These are merely choices, not commandments, and we encourage you to be open to the Holy Spirit's leading.

And to you group members, we would encourage you to bring along a small notebook where you can jot down insights you gain from others in your group, as well as work out your answers to the questions in advance. Happy growing!

---

1. We may not like to face it, but there's a little bit of Jacob in all of us. For example, do you tend to avoid conflict? Or, when confronted with difficult situations, do you rely more on your own cunning than on God?

2. We have discussed some of the obvious flaws of Jacob that contributed to the murderous hatred in the family. But what of Leah and Rachel, Zilpah and Bilhah? Were they passive as well? Read Genesis 29–31, 35, and identify the seeds of discontent sown by these women.

3. What will be the legacy you leave your children? Will it be a love for God and others? Jacob, Leah, Rachel, and the rest gifted their family with a mishmash of faith, love, deceit, jealousy, anxiety, and rage. Some good; much that wasn't. What legacy do you *want* to leave behind? What needs changing to begin moving you toward something better?

4. What parallels can you draw between the life of Joseph and Jesus? For example, both were misunderstood, both were rejected, both sold for money. Spend some time exploring these similarities from as many different perspectives as possible. Who did what? How did they feel? How did they respond?

5. Have you been or are you now going through any circumstances similar to what Joseph and Jesus endured? In what ways can you identify with them?

Chapter 2

RESISTING TEMPTATION
Genesis 39

In one of his best writings, a small booklet fewer than fifty pages long titled *Temptation*, Dietrich Bonhoeffer gave perhaps the single most descriptive explanation of temptation anywhere outside the Scriptures.

> In our members there is a slumbering inclination towards desire which is both sudden and fierce. With irresistible power, desire seizes mastery over the flesh. All at once a secret, smouldering fire is kindled. The flesh burns and is in flames. It makes no difference whether it is sexual desire, or ambition, or vanity, or desire for revenge, or love of fame and power, or greed for money or, finally, that strange desire for the beauty of the world, of nature. Joy in God is in course of being extinguished in us and we seek all our joy in the creature. At this moment God is quite unreal to us, he loses all reality, and only desire for the creature is real; the only reality is the devil. Satan does not here fill us with hatred of God, but with forgetfulness of God. . . . The lust thus aroused envelops the mind and will of man in deepest darkness. The powers of clear discrimination and of decision are taken from us. . . .
>
> It is here that everything within me rises up against the Word of God.[1]

Temptation is the oldest of all the inner conflicts in the human heart. There is not one person, including Christ, who hasn't struggled with it. And, except for Christ, there is not one person who hasn't suffered the consequences of yielding to it.

Three Types of Temptation

When it comes to temptation, we tend to make two assumptions.

---

1. Dietrich Bonhoeffer, *Creation and Fall* and *Temptation* (New York, N.Y.: Macmillan Publishing Co., Collier Books, 1959), pp. 116–17.

First, we assume that to be tempted is always a sin. However, Hebrews 4:15 teaches that, though temptation may lead to sin, it is not itself always a sin. Jesus, for example, was tempted, but He did not sin.

Second, we often think temptation is limited in its meaning to sexual lust. But there are many other ways in which we can be tempted. Let's look at two others as well as the sexual kind.

Material temptation. This is a lust for things. It can be something as large as a house or as small as a ring. Something as sleek and beautiful as a new car or as worn and nicked as an antique bureau.

Personal temptation. This is a lust for status. Some people expend all their energies trying to gain special recognition, fame, or power. They sacrifice friends, family—whatever gets in their way—to possess a title or a position.

Sensual temptation. This is the lust for physical pleasure. It may be the desire to enjoy the body of another individual when such pleasure is not legally or morally permissible.

Regardless of the kind of temptation, all of us know the frustration of trying to stop a Gulliver lust with a Lilliputian will.

In our lesson today we're going to look at Joseph's memorable example of how to resist the seductive enticements of a sensual temptation.

The Historic Situation

> Now Joseph had been taken down to Egypt; and Potiphar, an Egyptian officer of Pharaoh, the captain of the bodyguard, bought him from the Ishmaelites, who had taken him down there. The Lord was with Joseph, so he became a successful man. And he was in the house of his master, the Egyptian.[2] (Gen. 39:1–2)

In the first two verses, two things are conspicuous by their absence. First, there's no mention of how long Joseph has been Potiphar's slave before the events in this chapter take place. He may have been there a few months or a few years; we're not told.

Second, there's no mention of the traumatic adjustments Joseph has had to endure as a slave in a foreign land and culture. Remember, he is used to a doting old father and privileges that exempt him

---

2. Potiphar was an Egyptian grandee, who enjoyed title, wealth, and favor in Pharaoh's court. At times, he was also the royal executioner.

from menial tasks. Now he has to obey the commands of Pharaoh's chief officer and do *his* menial tasks.

But God's blessing is on Joseph's life, and this, coupled with Joseph's personal integrity and hard work, leads to his being promoted to a place of prominence.

> Now his master saw that the Lord was with him and how the Lord caused all that he did to prosper in his hand. So Joseph found favor in his sight and became his personal servant; and he made him overseer over his house, and all that he owned he put in his charge. (vv. 3–4)

Notice that Joseph didn't *tell* Potiphar that the Lord was with him; verse 3 says that "his master saw" that God was with him. And verse 4 says, "Joseph found favor in his [Potiphar's] sight," not "Joseph requested favors from Potiphar." Joseph earned the right to be respected and trusted.

> It came about that from the time he made him overseer in his house, and over all that he owned, the Lord blessed the Egyptian's house on account of Joseph; thus the Lord's blessing was upon all that he owned, in the house and in the field. So he left everything he owned in Joseph's charge; and with him there he did not concern himself with anything except the food which he ate. (vv. 5–6a)

By now, God's blessing combined with Joseph's personal integrity have inspired Potiphar's absolute confidence and trust. And along with that has come greater measures of responsibility and freedom for Joseph. But sneaking up behind these benefits also comes a greater measure of vulnerability. F. B. Meyer warns,

> *We may expect temptation in days of prosperity and ease* rather than in those of privation and toil . . . not where men frown, but where they smile sweet, exquisite smiles of flattery—it is there, it is there, that the temptress lies in wait! Beware! If thou goest armed anywhere, thou must, above all, go armed here.[3]

---

3. F. B. Meyer, *Joseph: Beloved—Hated—Exalted* (Fort Washington, Pa.: Christian Literature Crusade, n.d.), p. 30.

The writer of Genesis finishes this brief narrative of Joseph's professional life with a personal aside: "Now Joseph was handsome in form and appearance" (v. 6b).

The Sensual Temptation

While Mr. Potiphar is appreciating Joseph's reliable business sense and trustworthy nature, Mrs. Potiphar is becoming increasingly preoccupied with Joseph's good build and looks.

> It came about after these events that his master's wife looked with desire at Joseph, and she said, "Lie with me." (v. 7)

Joseph immediately but politely refuses. He tries to appeal to her reason first and then to her conscience.

> But he refused and said to his master's wife, "Behold, with me here, my master does not concern himself with anything in the house, and he has put all that he owns in my charge. There is no one greater in this house than I, and he has withheld nothing from me except you, because you are his wife. How then could I do this great evil and sin against God?" (vv. 8–9)

But Mrs. Potiphar isn't moved a bit. She isn't interested in the sanctity of her marriage or the trust between her husband and Joseph. She's interested only in gratifying her physical lust—*now.* Nothing else. It's no wonder, then, that Joseph's spiritual concern could not penetrate the darkness that shrouded her mind and will.

Peculiar Elements in Joseph's Temptation

Let's pause for just a moment to clarify some of the specifics in Joseph's situation. First, Joseph faced a difficult dilemma. The very place in which he lived and worked, Potiphar's household, brought him face-to-face with one very seductive temptation: Mrs. Potiphar. Second, her advances surely must have flattered Joseph's ego and aroused a powerful sensual temptation. Third, the source of temptation was persistent—she pursued him day after day (v. 10). Fourth, this woman pursued Joseph when they were alone, when there wouldn't be any fear of detection (v. 11).

It was a vulnerable time for Joseph. No doubt his own lust was working overtime trying to erode, as Bonhoeffer said, his powers of clear discrimination and decision (see also James 1:13–15).

The final test for Joseph came when Mrs. Potiphar resorted to more than just words to lure him to lie with her.

> She caught him by his garment, saying, "Lie with me!" And he left his garment in her hand and fled, and went outside. (Gen. 39:12)

In almost every instance where the issue of sexual lust is dealt with in the New Testament, we're told to flee, to get up and run (see 1 Cor. 6:18). Some temptations we're to stand and resist. But when it comes to sensual lust, we're told to do exactly as Joseph did—get out of there. If we stay, we're likely to give in.

The Personal Ramifications

William Congreve once said, "Heaven has no rage like love to hatred turned, Nor hell a fury like a woman scorned."[4] All the lust that has smoldered in Potiphar's wife suddenly blazes into fury. She wants revenge for her rejection.

> So she left his garment beside her until his master came home. Then she spoke to him with these words, "The Hebrew slave, whom you brought to us, came in to me to make sport of me; and as I raised my voice and screamed, he left his garment beside me and fled outside."
> Now when his master heard the words of his wife, which she spoke to him, saying, "This is what your slave did to me," his anger burned. So Joseph's master took him and put him into the jail, the place where the king's prisoners were confined; and he was there in the jail. (Gen. 39:16–20)

Joseph did the right thing. But once he got outside, he didn't hear any angels singing his praises for saying no. What he heard instead was the scream of a woman—a scream that would hurl him from the heights as Potiphar's overseer to the depths of an obscure jail cell.[5]

4. *Bartlett's Familiar Quotations*, 15th ed., rev. and enl., ed. Emily Morison Beck (Boston, Mass.: Little, Brown and Co., 1980), p. 324.

5. At first glance, Potiphar's reaction to his wife's story seems to indicate that he believed her. But when you read of Joseph's punishment, it suggests that his Egyptian master wasn't completely convinced. The normal sentence for a slave guilty of attempted rape was instant death. But Pharaoh's chief executioner kept his sword sheathed and put Joseph in prison instead. Was Potiphar mainly angry at having lost his best slave due to a wife he knew to be unfaithful?

The Practical Application for Today

Here are four important insights to help you say no when your lust says yes.

Do not be weakened by your situation. Several aspects of Joseph's position could easily have undercut his resolve to say no to lust. He was handsome and alone. He enjoyed a secure and trusted position. His integrity and accomplishments made him the object of much praise. And, perhaps, most dangerously, he had complete autonomy. He was accountable to no one. No one, that is, except God. Joseph did not allow his eyes to wander from his holy God to the sinful seductions of his situation.

Do not be deceived by persuasion. Mrs. Potiphar was bold and calculating, and her proposition was tantalizing. No doubt her verbal enticements were as loosely clad and suggestive as she probably was. Day after day she tried to lure Joseph with just the right combination of tempting words, such as, "My husband doesn't meet my needs." Or, "Who will ever find out? We're completely safe!" Or perhaps, "Just this once. What will it hurt?" But her words were in vain. Joseph's commitment to God completely shut her out.

Do not be gentle with your emotions. F. B. Meyer said, "Resist the first tiny thrill of temptation, lest it widen a breach big enough to admit the ocean. Remember that no temptation can master you unless you admit it *within*."[6] Our emotions will beg and plead for us to open the door to that first tiny thrill of temptation, but we've got to learn to keep the door closed like Joseph did. In verse 8 "he refused." In verse 9 he calls her words "this great evil, and a sin against God." In verse 10 he didn't even listen to her or stay near her. And in verse 12 he fled from her!

Do not be confused by the immediate results. Don't be confused when your "Mrs. Potiphars" keep coming back to tempt you after you've said no. Saying no to temptation, whatever kind it may be, doesn't banish it forever. Lust doesn't give up that easily. Be prepared to say no again the next day—or even the next minute.

---

6. Meyer, *Joseph*, p. 34.

Living Insights

The battle against temptation is a hard-fought one. Sometimes we gain a little ground one day, only to lose it and more the next. What can we do? Author Jerry Bridges shares a personal insight that revolutionized his resistance.

> One day as I was studying this chapter [1 John 2] I realized that my personal life's objective regarding holiness was less than that of John's. He was saying, in effect, "Make it your aim *not* to sin." As I thought about this, I realized that deep within my heart my real aim was not to sin *very much*. . . .
>
> Can you imagine a soldier going into battle with the aim of "not getting hit very much"? . . . We can be sure if that is our aim, we will be hit—not with bullets, but with temptation over and over again.[7]

What is your goal in the area of material, personal, and sensual temptation? Not to sin very much . . . or not to sin at all?

_____

_____

_____

Fortifying our internal attitude is critical, but we must also be careful how we walk—not as unwise people but as wise (Eph. 5:15). Think through each realm of temptation, and list any circumstances you need to avoid so you don't walk into an area land-mined with temptation.

Material _____

_____

Personal _____

_____

7. Jerry Bridges, *The Pursuit of Holiness* (Colorado Springs, Colo.: NavPress, 1978), p. 96.

Sensual _____

Questions for Group Discussion

1. Has temptation gained a beachhead in your life? How have you tried to regain control? How did Paul successfully deal with temptation (read Rom. 7:19–8:39)? In your own words, what does this really mean?

2. Billions of dollars are spent every year in the U.S. on marketing. How would you define what marketing is and does? For further insight, read 2 Peter 2:18–19. What marketing techniques have you seen or heard this past week alone? What did they appeal to? Was there an alluring temptation behind any of this for you?

3. Of the three areas of temptation identified in the lesson, are you tempted by one more than any other? Is it because you are being weakened by your situation? Deceived by persuasion? Too gentle with your emotions? Or confused by the immediate results?

4. Particularly in America, the enticement and pressure to sin is constant. Since temptation is unavoidable, what can we do to prepare our children and especially our young teens for the on-slaught (read Phil. 3:17–20)? For further study, see Proverbs 1–10.

5. Drawing from Joseph's response to Potiphar's wife (Gen. 39:8–9), what motivated him to resist so seductive a temptation? What have you found to be of little help in a time of temptation?

6. The price tag for Joseph's integrity was high. What would you be willing to give up for the sake of your personal purity? What's the worst that might happen? Not taking a stand is taking a stand all the same. What happens in the meantime to your character and relationship with God?

Chapter 3

IMPRISONED AND FORGOTTEN
Genesis 39:20–41:1

Aleksandr Solzhenitsyn and Elie Wiesel. Both men represent millions of other men, women, and children who have been imprisoned and forgotten by humanity. People who suffered unjustly in Russian gulags or Nazi concentration camps. For some, like Solzhenitsyn, these man-made hells helped bring about their spiritual conversion. For others, like Wiesel, the hellish experience reduced what faith they had to a scorched cinder.

> Never shall I forget that night, the first night in camp, which has turned my life into one long night, seven times cursed and seven times sealed. Never shall I forget that smoke. Never shall I forget the little faces of the children, whose bodies I saw turned into wreaths of smoke beneath a silent blue sky.
>
> Never shall I forget those flames which consumed my faith forever.
>
> Never shall I forget that nocturnal silence which deprived me, for all eternity, of the desire to live. Never shall I forget those moments which murdered my God and my soul and turned my dreams to dust. Never shall I forget these things, even if I am condemned to live as long as God Himself. Never.[1]

The pain of suffering unjustly is one of the severest trials we can enter into. It is a sanctuary of flames from which some emerge with a tempered, unshakable faith; while others, only ashes.

It is also inescapable. Every day children are stolen, abused, and aborted. Wives are battered. Spouses are abandoned by unfaithful partners. Drunk drivers maim and kill. Gossip and slander ruin reputations.

The greatest test in this kind of suffering is our attitude toward it. Viktor Frankl wrote,

Everything can be taken from a man but one thing:

---

1. Elie Wiesel, *Night*, trans. Stella Rodway (New York, N.Y.: Bantam Books, 1960), p. 32.

the last of the human freedoms—to choose one's attitude in any given set of circumstances, to choose one's own way.[2]

We cannot control whether today or tomorrow we will be treated fairly. But we can choose how we will respond. Our attitude is something we can control. Resentment, hostility, bitterness, revenge—these are the common attitudes people choose when they're mistreated. God, however, has a different choice in mind for His children.

> For what credit is there if, when you sin and are harshly treated, you endure it with patience? But if when you do what is right and suffer for it you patiently endure it, this finds favor with God. (1 Pet. 2:20)

Joseph did what was right, and he suffered for it. He refused Mrs. Potiphar's advances, so she concocted a lie that sent him to prison. From free man to slave to prisoner, Joseph's freedom was progressively stripped away. Everything about his circumstances seemed to indicate that he had been forgotten by both God and people. Now Joseph faced the greatest test. Now he had to exercise the only freedom left to him—the freedom to choose his attitude.

Before we see how Joseph responded, let's take a brief look at the different ways we all suffer unjustly.

Mistreatment: Common to Everyone

We all experience three basic kinds of mistreatment.

Undeserved treatment from family. Even in the best of families you won't escape pain, because parents aren't perfect and neither are brothers and sisters.

Unexpected restrictions from circumstances. Mistreatment confines us either physically or emotionally. We may be in a situation where we can't fight back or change things. And these unexpected restrictions are painful.

Untrue accusations from people. James aptly describes the tongue as a fire (James 3:5–6). In one day its careless, untrue statements can completely incinerate a reputation that has taken years to build.

2. Viktor E. Frankl, *Man's Search for Meaning,* rev. and updated (New York, N.Y.: Pocket Books, 1984), p. 86.

Imprisonment: Joseph in Jail

If you've ever wondered whether the Bible deals with real-life situations, the story of Joseph should dispel any doubts. We've only studied two chapters in his biography so far, and already he has experienced all three categories of mistreatment: his brothers hated him and sold him into slavery, he was confined as someone else's slave, and he was falsely accused by his master's wife. Once again Joseph was thrown from a privileged position into a pit—only this time, instead of a dry well in Dothan, it was a dark dungeon in Egypt (Gen. 39:20).

Where Is God in All of This?

It's usually easy to see God in the good things that happen to us. But what about when something unfair happens, like Joseph being thrown into prison—where is God now? Genesis 39:21 tells us, "The Lord [is] with Joseph." He has never left him. Furthermore, the Lord "[extends] kindness to him, and [gives] him favor in the sight of the chief jailer" (v. 21).

What Happened?

It would have been so easy, it would have felt so right, for Joseph to become bitter and vengeful. But he *chooses*, instead, to patiently endure prison. And the Lord gives him an inner peace, as well as favor in the eyes of those around him. As in Potiphar's house before, Joseph's attitude makes him a useful tool in God's hands.

> The chief jailer committed to Joseph's charge all the prisoners who were in the jail; so that whatever was done there, he was responsible for it. . . . And whatever he did, the Lord made to prosper. (vv. 22, 23b)

First and foremost in Joseph's life is his trust in God. And if God has chosen to allow him to be put in prison, Joseph sees that as His sovereign right. He doesn't argue with God or take it personally. Instead, he recognizes that God's hand is in it and humbly approaches his new restriction as another opportunity for God to work in his life. Because of that, God is able to use him strategically in the lives of two men.

> Then it came about after these things, the cup-bearer and the baker for the king of Egypt offended their lord, the king of Egypt. Pharaoh was furious

with his two officials, the chief cupbearer and the chief baker. So he put them in confinement in the house of the captain of the bodyguard, in the jail, the same place where Joseph was imprisoned. The captain of the bodyguard put Joseph in charge of them, and he took care of them; and they were in confinement for some time. (40:1–4)

We're not told what these men have done to offend Pharaoh, but chances are, given their former job titles, it has something to do with Pharaoh's food. The baker obviously had prepared his meals, and it had been the cupbearer's job to taste Pharaoh's food and wine to prevent him from being poisoned.

Then the cupbearer and the baker for the king of Egypt, who were confined in jail, both had a dream the same night, each man with his own dream and each dream with its own interpretation. When Joseph came to them in the morning and observed them, behold, they were dejected. He asked Pharaoh's officials who were with him in confinement in his master's house, "Why are your faces so sad today?" (vv. 5–7)

Even though the bottom has dropped out of his life, Joseph's attitude of patient endurance enables him to be sensitive to the needs of others. And it is this concern for others that starts a chain of events that will eventually lead to his release, beginning with the interpretation of the king's servants' dreams.

Then they said to him, "We have had a dream and there is no one to interpret it." Then Joseph said to them, "Do not interpretations belong to God? Tell it to me, please." (v. 8)

If you'll remember, Joseph has had some experience with dreams before, and all it had done was create problems for him (see 37:5–11). Yet when he hears that these men are upset because no one can interpret their dreams, he still offers to help.

The First Dream

So the chief cupbearer told his dream to Joseph, and said to him, "In my dream, behold, there was a vine in front of me; and on the vine were three branches. And as it was budding, its blossoms came out, and its clusters produced ripe grapes. Now Pharaoh's cup was in my hand; so I took the grapes and squeezed them into Pharaoh's cup, and I put the cup into Pharaoh's hand." Then Joseph said to him, "This is the interpretation of it: the three branches are three days; within three more days Pharaoh will lift up your head and restore you to your office; and you will put Pharaoh's cup into his hand according to your former custom when you were his cupbearer." (40:9–13)

No doubt this is exciting news for the cupbearer. And Joseph sees the possibility of something good in it for himself too. The next two verses remind us that Joseph was a real flesh-and-blood human being, not some pristine saint whose feet never touched the ground.

"Only keep me in mind when it goes well with you, and please do me a kindness by mentioning me to Pharaoh and get me out of this house. For I was in fact kidnapped from the land of the Hebrews, and even here I have done nothing that they should have put me into the dungeon." (vv. 14–15)

The Second Dream

After hearing the cupbearer's good fortune, the baker immediately launches into his dream. And Joseph faces the unpleasant task of having to tell him that his wasn't a dream—it was a nightmare.

When the chief baker saw that he had interpreted favorably, he said to Joseph, "I also saw in my dream, and behold, there were three baskets of white bread on my head; and in the top basket there were some of all sorts of baked food for Pharaoh, and the birds were eating them out of the basket on my head." Then Joseph answered and said, "This is its interpretation: the three baskets are three days; within three more days Pharaoh will lift up your head from you and will hang you on a tree, and the birds will eat your flesh off you." (vv. 16–19)

Expectation

Three days later everything happens just as Joseph has said. The cupbearer goes back to serving Pharaoh, and the baker becomes food for the birds (vv. 20–22). While he must hate to see such a dire interpretation come true, all of this must also raise some hopeful expectations in Joseph. In his daydreams he can probably see the cupbearer convincing Pharaoh to free him. Mentally, Joseph has his bags packed and is ready to go.

Abandonment: Joseph Forgotten

There is only one problem though. The cupbearer has a short memory.

> Yet the chief cupbearer did not remember Joseph,
> but forgot him.
> Now it happened at the end of two full years
> that Pharaoh had a dream. (40:23–41:1a)

There are two important observations we should mention here about Joseph's situation. First, *he was abandoned by a friend*. If an enemy abandons you, who cares? But when it's a friend, that cuts deep. Second, *the abandonment was for a lengthy period of time*. Sometimes we get upset when we're neglected even for a minute. According to 41:1, Joseph was abandoned for two years.

Earlier, we said there are three different types of mistreatment. But from this part of Joseph's life we can add another: *Unfair abandonment from one you helped*. All of us can identify with this. Perhaps you've been left by a mate for whom you worked and sacrificed to put through school. Or maybe you started a business with a partner, someone you trusted, only to find out this person has been siphoning off the company's profits.

Our natural response to this kind of an experience is to feel disillusioned, betrayed—first with the person who abandoned us, then with God. If we keep replaying those scenes, we allow our feelings to fester. And they will begin to harden our hearts with bitterness.

Encouragement: God Is There

Feelings of disillusionment, however, need not last forever. Joseph may have been initially disappointed by his cellmate's forgetfulness, but he didn't sink into a pit of angry despair. His hope and trust were ultimately in God, whose care never falters and whose plans never fail.

It's true, everything can be taken from us except that one precious freedom to choose our attitude—because the basis of our attitude is a trustworthy God. With God on our side, all the mistreatment the world has to offer need not reduce our hope to the ashes of disillusionment.

Living Insights

For all Joseph knew and felt, prison was going to be his permanent home. Has there been a time in your life, perhaps even now, when your circumstances felt unending? When the psalmist's bitter cry became your own?

> My God, my God, why have You forsaken me?
> Far from my deliverance are the words of my
>   groaning.
> O my God, I cry by day, but You do not answer;
> And by night, but I have no rest. (Ps. 22:1–2)

Surely in the darkness of that prison cell Joseph must have shaken his fist in anger and cried tears of loneliness and loss. Yet his anger did not last; he did not abandon God or forget his faith. What kept Joseph from going over the edge?

Could it have had something to do with where Joseph ultimately placed his trust? Read through Psalm 146:3–5, and consider how the psalmist's words were reflected in Joseph's life. How can they shine through your life?

_____

_____

_____

_____

The next time you feel forgotten, forsaken, or disillusioned, remember that there is One who is trustworthy, and He has not forsaken or forgotten you. Here are a few heavenly reminders to strengthen your heart to believe, your eyes to see, your mind to understand His trustworthiness, even in the darkest of nights.

The Trustworthiness of God

Deuteronomy 31:6	Isaiah 42:16
Psalm 37:3–6, 28	Matthew 28:20b
Psalm 118:5–9	Hebrews 13:5
Proverbs 3:5–6	1 Peter 5:6–7

 Questions for Group Discussion

1. Are you enduring mistreatment right now? Are you feeling angry about it? Is that wrong? Are you expressing that anger in ways that are appropriate, healthy, and healing, or in ways that cause more hurt, anger, and alienation?

2. Have thoughts of revenge crossed your mind? Have you ever acted on those vengeful thoughts? What were the consequences? What does God have to say about this (see Rom. 12:17–21)?

3. Have you grown weary of doing good? It's not always easy, especially when your good deeds are not reciprocated. What can keep you going? For further study, read Galatians 6:9; 2 Thessalonians 3:13.

4. Some people abandon the faith because of mistreatment. "A pastor lied to me once, so I quit going to church and haven't been back since." How would you respond to such a person?

5. As F. B. Meyer observed, "Though stripped of his coat, [Joseph] had not been stripped of his character."[3] Whether in Potiphar's house or in prison, Joseph worked in a way that pleased God and caught the eye of his master. Pause for a moment to read Colossians 3:23–24 and 1 Peter 4:10–11. Now consider this: Who do you work for, in public or private, at home or in a large corporate office, whether noticed or unnoticed, appreciated or ignored? Who are you trying to please?

6. All of us have been mistreated at one time or another. What were some of the practical ways others comforted you during that time? Is there someone near you who needs some of that same comfort (see 2 Cor. 1:3–4)?

---

3. F. B. Meyer, *Joseph: Beloved—Hated—Exalted* (Fort Washington, Pa.: Christian Literature Crusade, n.d.), p. 27.

Chapter 4

REMEMBERED AND PROMOTED

Genesis 41:1–46

Of all the different categories of truth in the Bible, none are more helpful than God's promises—all 7,487 of them.[1] Promises like:

"Can a woman forget her nursing child
And have no compassion on the son of her womb?
Even these may forget, but I will not forget you.
Behold, I have inscribed you on the palms of
My hands." (Isa. 49:15–16)

Jesus said to her, "I am the resurrection and the life;
he who believes in Me will live even if he dies."
(John 11:25)

Of all the promises, though, none are more meaningful than those that promise divine blessing after human suffering, hope after affliction. Let's take a moment to look at some examples of this kind of promise from both the Old and New Testaments.

Promises of Divine Promotion

Tucked away in the Old Testament is a book that reads like a chronicle of calamity. It is named for its main character, Job, and details how he was assaulted by loss, disease, grief, and misguided friends. In chapter 23, Job wants the *why* and *how long* questions answered. He wants an opportunity to argue his innocence before God and end his pain. But he cannot present his case because he cannot find the Judge (vv. 3–4, 8–9). In the midst of this long, dark night of suffering, though, Job reminds himself of a fact, a

---

1. Herbert Lockyer, *All the Promises of the Bible* (Grand Rapids, Mich.: Zondervan Publishing House, 1962), p. 10. Lockyer records the story of a man named Everet R. Storms who, during his twenty-seventh reading of the Bible, broke down the promises of Scripture as follows: "7,487 promises by God to man, 2 by God the Father to God the Son, 991 by one man to another . . . , 290 by man to God. 21 promises were made by angels, one by man to an angel, and two were made by an evil spirit to the Lord. Satan made nine. . . . Storms then gives us the grand total of 8,810 promises."

promise, a hope:

> "But He knows the way I take;
> When He has tried me, I shall come forth as gold."
> (v. 10)

Notice Job said, "*When* He has tried me," which implies the passage of time. There's no such thing as a quick way to refine gold. The process of refining, purifying, and perfecting gold is a lengthy, painstaking process. In the same way, God uses the painstaking process of our afflictions and sufferings to refine and perfect His character in us.

Over in the New Testament the same kind of promise is anchored amidst some intense affliction in 1 Peter 5. According to verse 6, something was happening that prompted Peter to remind his readers to *humble* themselves and not resist God. Verse 7 addresses feelings of *anxiety*. Verse 8 talks about the enemy, the devil, wanting to *devour* them. And verse 9 plainly states that they were going through some kind of *suffering*, though what it is isn't explicitly stated. Finally, in verse 10 comes the promise that can keep all our lives from being capsized by troubles.

> After you have suffered for a little while, the God of all grace, who called you to His eternal glory in Christ, will Himself perfect, confirm, strengthen and establish you. (v. 10)

When the testing has ended, when the flames have consumed the dross of self-centeredness, you'll come forth as gold. However, keep in mind that what Peter is saying has nothing to do with externals— and neither did Job's example. Job did not say, "When He has tried me, He'll double the wealth He took away," or, "When He has tried me, my wife will turn around and say she's sorry, and our relationship will be better than before." No, he reflected Peter's truth and said, "I'll come forth as gold; I'll be wiser, purer, more like Him."

So don't resist trials and afflictions as intruders. Rather, submit to God in the midst of them, allowing Him to perfect, confirm, strengthen, and establish your character for His purposes.

The Test: Darkness before Dawn

In our last study, we saw that Joseph's new friend, Pharaoh's cupbearer, promptly forgot about him for the next two years (41:1).

Why did God let that happen? Because He wasn't through with the gold-making process. Joseph wasn't quite ready to handle the promotion that God was preparing for him.

What happened during those two years? Nothing . . . on the outside. Joseph lived out monotonous hours that stacked up into days, months, and finally years. Humanly speaking, waiting is one of the most difficult tasks we can be assigned. From our perspective it feels like we're stagnating and getting nowhere. But, from God's perspective, it is the ideal crucible for strengthening and establishing His character in us.

The Turning Point: Pharaoh's Dream

Ironically, the turning point in Joseph's life came as a result of another dream.

The Dream Declared

Pharaoh woke up one morning disturbed over two strange dreams. He had first dreamed that there were seven fat, sleek cows who came up out of the Nile and were followed by seven gaunt, ugly cows who devoured them. After this, he dreamed of seven plump, good ears of grain growing on a single stalk, which were then swallowed up by seven thin, scorched ears (Gen. 41:1–7). When Pharaoh awoke, he called for all his magicians and wise men to interpret these dreams for him (v. 8). But none of them could. Suddenly, the cupbearer remembers another interpreter of dreams and immediately begins to pour out a long-forgotten favor.

> Then the chief cupbearer spoke to Pharaoh, saying, "I would make mention today of my own offenses. Pharaoh was furious with his servants, and he put me in confinement in the house of the captain of the bodyguard, both me and the chief baker. We had a dream on the same night, he and I; each of us dreamed according to the interpretation of his own dream. Now a Hebrew youth was with us there, a servant of the captain of the bodyguard, and we related them to him, and he interpreted our dreams for us. To each one he interpreted according to his own dream. And just as he interpreted for us, so it happened; he restored me in my office, but he hanged him." (vv. 9–13)

29

The Dream Interpreted

Pharaoh immediately calls to have Joseph brought up from prison. Hurriedly he is made to shave and change clothes (v. 14).

Just for a moment, put yourself in Joseph's sandals. Why has he been down in that furnace called a dungeon for the past two years? Humanly speaking, it was because the cupbearer forgot him. Now, suddenly, he's released and standing in front of Pharaoh, the cupbearer's boss. But you won't hear one word of resentment spoken against the cupbearer. Why? Because Joseph kept his eyes on the Lord, not the cupbearer.

> Pharaoh said to Joseph, "I have had a dream, but no one can interpret it; and I have heard it said about you, that when you hear a dream you can interpret it." Joseph then answered Pharaoh, saying, "It is not in me; God will give Pharaoh a favorable answer." (vv. 15–16)

The New International Version says, "I cannot do it." Joseph isn't nitpicking over terms here. He wants it clearly understood that if truth comes, it will come from God, and He alone deserves the glory. The years of suffering have purged him, and now he has come forth as gold—having the kind of character that refuses to use God's gift of interpreting dreams as a bargaining chip to secure his freedom.

Pharaoh then tells Joseph his dreams (vv. 17–24), and Joseph explains that God was telling Pharaoh what He is about to do. The seven fat cows and the seven plump ears of grain represent seven years of great abundance throughout Egypt. This bumper crop will then be followed by seven years of famine, which in the dream were represented by the gaunt cows and thin grain swallowing up the good. This famine will be so intense that the people will forget there were ever days of plenty (vv. 25–31). Even to the end of the interpretation, Joseph keeps Pharaoh's focus on the Lord and off himself.

> "Now as for the repeating of the dream to Pharaoh twice, it means that the matter is determined by God, and God will quickly bring it about." (v. 32)

Pharaoh was powerful, but even the world's greatest army was defenseless against the onslaught of a famine. At this moment of weakness, Joseph provided Pharaoh with the battle plan he needed to save the Egyptian empire from ruin.

"Now let Pharaoh look for a man discerning and wise, and set him over the land of Egypt. Let Pharaoh take action to appoint overseers in charge of the land, and let him exact a fifth of the produce of the land of Egypt in the seven years of abundance. Then let them gather all the food of these good years that are coming, and store up the grain for food in the cities under Pharaoh's authority, and let them guard it. Let the food become as a reserve for the land for the seven years of famine which will occur in the land of Egypt, so that the land will not perish during the famine." (vv. 33–36)

The Reward: Joseph's Promotion

When Joseph counseled Pharaoh, he spoke directly, honestly, and for God's glory. He wasn't interviewing for a job. But the refined qualities of discernment and humility shone through in what he was saying, and they caught Pharaoh's eye.

Honored for His Character

Now the proposal seemed good to Pharaoh and to all his servants. Then Pharaoh said to his servants, "Can we find a man like this, in whom is a divine spirit?" So Pharaoh said to Joseph, "Since God has informed you of all this, there is no one so discerning and wise as you are." (vv. 37–39)

The word *discerning* here means the ability to have shrewd insight into a situation and its needs. And the wisdom Joseph displayed assured Pharaoh that he had this kind of deep perception. So in a stunning reversal, Joseph is given a promotion that will take him in one day from the pit to the pinnacle of Egypt.

Exalted over Egypt

"You shall be over my house, and according to your command all my people shall do homage; only in the throne I will be greater than you." Pharaoh said to Joseph, "See, I have set you over all the land of Egypt." Then Pharaoh took off his signet ring from his hand and put it on Joseph's hand, and clothed him in garments of fine linen and put the gold neck-lace around his neck. He had him ride in his second chariot; and they proclaimed before him, "Bow the knee!" And he set him over all the land of Egypt. (vv. 40–43)

As F. B. Meyer writes,

> It was a wonderful ascent, sheer in a single bound from the dungeon to the steps of the throne. His father had rebuked him; now Pharaoh, the greatest monarch of his time, welcomes him. . . . The hands that were hard with the toils of a slave are adorned with a signet ring. The feet are no longer tormented by fetters; a chain of gold is linked around his neck. The coat of many colours torn from him by violence and defiled by blood, and the garment left in the hand of the adulteress, are exchanged for vestures of fine linen drawn from the royal wardrobe. He was once trampled upon as the offscouring of all things; now all Egypt is commanded to bow before him, as he rides forth in the second chariot, prime minister of Egypt, and second only to the king.[2]

Responses We Can Learn from Joseph

Joseph's Cinderella promotion was incredible. But let's not end our study focusing on the gold necklace he wore and forgetting the gold character it adorned.

That character was made possible by two important responses—responses that are not exclusive to Joseph.

First: *During the waiting period, trust God without panic.* We must learn to count on Him to handle the cupbearers of our lives who may forget and abandon us. Second: *During the time of reward, thank God without pride.* Oftentimes the night of our suffering seems as if it will never pass. We feel as if we can't even remember what the dawn was like. In our hearts, we pray for endurance and promise to thank God and give Him the glory when the dawn comes. But that thankfulness, that humility, often vanishes like morning mist when God rewards us. The best way to guard against this is to thank Him—continually—even during the dungeon times (see Eph. 5:15–20).

2. F. B. Meyer, *Joseph: Beloved—Hated—Exalted* (Fort Washington, Pa.: Christian Literature Crusade, n.d.), p. 62.

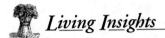 *Living Insights*

The dross of our character—pride, rebellion, self-sufficiency—melts in the crucible called waiting. Yet it is a crucible that we do everything to avoid. We even have a cultural myth that says to wait is to waste time. "Got to keep busy, on the move, doing." And even though suffering may force us to slow down, to wait, we complain and seek solace in mindless distractions and miss the refining of our character that God intended.

Do you look at waiting as a waste of time? Perhaps it would encourage you to grasp even just a glimpse of the why behind your waiting. First Peter 5:10 says that God will "perfect, confirm, strengthen and establish you." Pause to pray that God will help you see His work in your character with the following questions.

What will He perfect? _____

_____

_____

_____

Confirm? _____

_____

_____

_____

Strengthen? _____

_____

_____

_____

Establish? _____

_____

_____

_____

"When He has tried me, I shall come forth as gold" (Job 23:10). What do you think—is the waiting worth it?

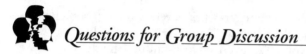 *Questions for Group Discussion*

1. In the darkness of our dungeon experiences, we think that we will never cease to be thankful if remembered and promoted by God. But experience proves that when it comes to gratitude, we all seem to have poor memories. Joseph's father, Jacob, practiced a very simple solution for this human frailty. Take a moment to read Genesis 33:18–20; 35:7, 14–15. What are some physical reminders (traditions, for example) you can develop to help remember God's goodness?

2. None of us can escape the influence of the culture we live in. Somehow, prolonged waiting and suffering like Joseph's just don't fit into the American Dream. What else of Joseph's experience doesn't fit with the American Dream?

3. What Americanisms are woven into the fabric of our thinking as Christians? For example: "If you're good, then you'll be rewarded" (Joseph was "good" but it landed him in prison). "God helps those who help themselves" (Joseph asked the cupbearer to remember him and he spent two more years in prison). What are some other examples?

4. Mother Teresa was known for her compassion. Former president Jimmy Carter is known for his care for the poor and homeless through Habitat for Humanity. Joseph was immediately recognized by Pharaoh for his divine discernment and wisdom. What are you known for? What do people immediately recognize about you, aside from where you work, what car you drive, or anything else external? Where did this come from; how did it develop?

5. What appeals to you most from what you've seen in Joseph thus far? Is it his patience? His integrity? His faith in God? His humility? His ability to forgive and not take revenge? After you choose, ask yourself why this is so appealing, and see how it connects with where you are or what you've been through.

Chapter 5

REAPING THE REWARDS OF RIGHTEOUSNESS
Genesis 41:41–57

On a scale of one to ten, ten being the highest, how positive and affirming are you? Are the private and public conversations you carry on with others edifying? Would you say you're a Corrie ten Boom *two*? One way of finding out is to give yourself the following two tests.

First, think about how encouraging you are when other people are afflicted, depressed, crushed. Do you weep with those who weep?

Second, reflect on how affirming you are when someone is suddenly promoted and becomes prosperous. Do you rejoice with those who rejoice? Curiously, many of us gravitate toward being critical rather than joyful, suspicious rather than supportive.

Someone most of us are used to envisioning in difficult circumstances is the apostle Paul. According to 2 Corinthians 11:23–27, he received thirty-nine lashes five times; he was beaten with rods three times, stoned once, and shipwrecked three times; and he was threatened by a host of other dangers on occasions too numerous to mention. But Paul also told the Philippians that not every day of his life was spent enduring some affliction.

> I have learned to be content in whatever circumstances I am. I know how to get along with humble means, and I also know how to live in prosperity; in any and every circumstance I have learned the secret of being filled and going hungry, both of having abundance and suffering need. (Phil. 4:11b–12)

Paul having abundance? Most of us can picture him in pain as a half-starved saint, but as a rejoicing well-fed one? No. That's one picture many of us have been conditioned not to see. Why?

The truth is, we persistently compare the suffering days with the prosperous and say the first is spiritual and the other is carnal. As a result, we tend to be more affirming of those living with humble means and suffering need than we are of those who live in prosperity and have an abundance.

A Brief Review

As we travel back to Joseph's biography in Genesis, let's add to the relevance of our study by imagining Joseph as a contemporary Christian friend. Now, so far, this friend has been through some very difficult days. He was hated and rejected by his own brothers, sold to a passing caravan, and later sold again on the slave's auction block in Egypt. Removed from and forgotten by his family, Joseph was forced to learn a new language and culture under the command of Potiphar, the captain of Pharaoh's bodyguard. Meanwhile, Mrs. Potiphar tried repeatedly to seduce Joseph, and when she finally saw that he wouldn't succumb, she falsely accused him of attempted rape. This charge landed him in prison, where he was forgotten by a friend who could possibly have secured his release two years earlier.

Joseph had suffered deeply. But he continued to walk with God through all this. Which of us wouldn't have rallied around him with all the encouragement we could give? "I'm praying for you." "You did the right thing, Joseph." "Keep trusting in the Lord; He hasn't forgotten you!"

In the last seventeen verses of Genesis 41, however, Joseph's life is going to be radically reversed, and he will face the difficult test of success. How supportive will we be when our friend Joseph is suddenly promoted? Let's find out.

A Man Restored

As we saw in our last lesson, Joseph was unexpectedly brought before Pharaoh to interpret two dreams that had troubled the king. In addition, Joseph offered Pharaoh some invaluable counsel that would save the Egyptian empire from ruin. Because of Joseph's discernment and wisdom, Pharaoh immediately promoted him from prisoner to prime minister. And with that promotion came many rewards.

A Position of Great Authority

One by one, Pharaoh bestows on Joseph several kinds of authority. First, he receives unlimited territorial authority: "I have set you over all the land of Egypt" (Gen. 41:41b). The whole land is to be under Joseph's control—a land richly nourished by the Nile and covered with cities, stately temples, pyramids, and colossal figures towering over one hundred feet in height.

Pharaoh also gives Joseph carte blanche financial authority: "Then Pharaoh took off his signet ring from his hand and put it on Joseph's hand" (v. 42a). The term *signet ring* comes from the Hebrew verb that means "to sink down." The ring was used for sinking the Pharaoh's emblem into soft clay. It was like the MasterCard of that day, with all the wealth of Egypt behind it. And now it belongs to Joseph, to make any transaction he deems necessary.

Joseph also receives a whole new wardrobe to match the new royal authority given him. The prison garments are quickly thrown away and replaced with "garments of fine linen" and a necklace made of gold (v. 42b).

Next, Joseph is given his own company car, Pharaoh's "second chariot," to be driven throughout Egypt to proclaim the new prime minister's public authority.

> He had him ride in his second chariot; and they proclaimed before him, "Bow the knee!" And he set him over all the land of Egypt. Moreover, Pharaoh said to Joseph, "Though I am Pharaoh, yet without your permission no one shall raise his hand or foot in all the land of Egypt." (vv. 43–44)

Now, if Joseph's newly acquired territorial and financial authority didn't bother you, seeing him surrounded by soldiers shouting for everyone to bow the knee and show respect probably does. It's hard to be affirming of that kind of success. We tend to look with a jaundiced eye and ask, "Who does he think he is?"

But the Scriptures never once say that Joseph commanded anyone to bow the knee. In fact, Joseph was probably embarrassed by all the hoopla and overwhelmed by the incredible irony of the situation. For there he was, a Hebrew as Egypt's new prime minister, riding in Pharaoh's chariot with the scars of slavery still on him.

New Name, New Wife

In addition to his new authority, Joseph is also given a new name—Zaphenath-paneah (v. 45a). The small syllable *nath* is a reference to a goddess worshiped in Egypt named Neith. Translated, Pharaoh's new name for Joseph means "the god speaks and lives." Certainly this is not the kind of name Joseph would choose for himself. But, as he is quickly finding out, some things aren't yours to determine when someone else promotes you to a position of authority.

To promote his social standing in Egypt, Joseph is also given a wife: "Asenath, the daughter of Potiphera priest of On" (v. 45b). Her name, which also includes the syllable *nath*, means "belonging to Neith." We're not told whether she is bright or dull, attractive or plain, sympathetic to Joseph's faith or antagonistic. Only that she is the daughter of an Egyptian priest.

Youth and a Bright Future

The writer pauses in verse 46 to tell us a significant personal fact about Joseph. This former Hebrew slave who now rules Egypt is only thirty years old.

So often we think God blesses and uses only older men and women in leadership positions. The Bible, however, is filled with examples of young leaders. Do you know how old David was when Samuel anointed him to be Israel's next king? Not even twenty. When Nebuchadnezzar picked Daniel to serve in his court, he was still in his teens. And Josiah, in 2 Chronicles 34, was only eight years old when he began his reign in Jerusalem.[1]

Joseph was a young man with a very promising future. He had been assured by God that, for the next seven years, Egypt would be blessed with unprecedented bumper crops. And it was.

> Thus Joseph stored up grain in great abundance like
> the sand of the sea, until he stopped measuring it,
> for it was beyond measure. (v. 49)

Now, on a scale of one to ten, would you still be praying for Joseph as intensely as you had before, when he was still in prison? Would you still affirm this richly adorned young man who rode in Pharaoh's chariot? Would you still be supportive of someone who was named "the god speaks and lives" and who was married to the daughter of a pagan priest? To be honest, many of us would probably score only about a one or two on the scale. But we are looking only at the surface. Let's find out what Joseph was like on the inside at this time.

Two Sons and a Clear Conscience

In the next few verses, Joseph uses a play on words that reveals his heart attitude toward God.

> Now before the year of famine came, two sons
> were born to Joseph, whom Asenath, the daughter

---

1. There is no lack of evidence outside the Bible either. Charles Haddon Spurgeon took the pulpit of New Park Street Chapel while still in his teens. Before he was thirty, six thousand people were coming each week to the famed London Tabernacle to hear him preach. And another famous preacher, G. Campbell Morgan, was only twelve when he gave his first sermon.

of Potiphera priest of On, bore to him. Joseph named the firstborn Manasseh, "For," he said, "God has made me forget all my trouble and all my father's household." He named the second Ephraim, "For," he said, "God has made me fruitful in the land of my affliction." (vv. 50–52)

The latter part of verse 51 actually reads, "God Manassehed me of all my troubles and all my father's household." What does this mean? The root of the word Manasseh is *nashah*, meaning "to forget." But in the Hebrew construction of this word, Manasseh means "to take the sting out of a memory." Joseph had many painful memories from his troublesome past. But with the birth of his first son, God removed the sting, so Joseph named his firstborn Manasseh.

Ephraim comes from the verb meaning "to be fruitful." The name of this second son was to be a living reminder and testimony that it was God who "Ephraimed" Joseph, made him fruitful in the land of his affliction. Underneath the exterior trappings of Egyptian royalty beat a heart that was still committed to "bowing the knee" to Jehovah.

Food amidst Famine

The integrity of Joseph's faith and character is also revealed in verses 53–57.

> When the seven years of plenty which had been in the land of Egypt came to an end, and the seven years of famine began to come, just as Joseph had said, then there was famine in all the lands, but in all the land of Egypt there was bread. So when all the land of Egypt was famished, the people cried out to Pharaoh for bread; and Pharaoh said to all the Egyptians, "Go to Joseph; whatever he says to you, you shall do." When the famine was spread over all the face of the earth, then Joseph opened all the storehouses, and sold to the Egyptians; and the famine was severe in the land of Egypt. The people of all the earth came to Egypt to buy grain from Joseph, because the famine was severe in all the earth.

Because Joseph believed God's prediction and was faithful in the execution of his job, Egypt and all the world benefited. Untold thousands survived the famine who otherwise would have perished.

A Word of Hope

On the surface, it wouldn't appear as if many of us have much in common with the Joseph of Genesis 41:41–57. You'll probably never be given the kind of territorial, financial, or public authority he received. It's likely you'll drive to work each day in your own car instead of being picked up by a presidential chariot. No one, not even your best friend, is going to run out in front of you telling people, "Bow the knee!" And what about the clothes Joseph wore? They were designer-royalty linens from Pharaoh's own private haberdashery. And yours?

Don't be too concerned, however, if you don't share all the same exterior trappings as Joseph. The clothes, the chariot—they're all dust anyway. Focus instead on these timeless interior lessons from Joseph's heart.

First: *Lengthy afflictions need not discourage us.* So much of our attention has been focused on what happened to Joseph that many of you may have missed the timing involved. Remember that Joseph was only seventeen when the bottom fell out of his life, and it wasn't until he was thirty that his circumstances significantly improved. Thirteen years of unrelenting affliction! And yet Joseph didn't allow discouragement to imprison his heart and make him lose hope. How did he do it? The only way possible—he focused on loving God with all his heart, soul, mind, and strength.

Second: *Bad memories need not defeat us.* The past is still present within us in the form of memories. And for many, painful memories are still what's controlling and defeating our attempts to love God and others. But we *can* free ourselves from them. By God's grace, we have the power to choose whom we will serve—a bad memory or a loving God. You may need some help at first, maybe from a friend, a close-knit fellowship group, or even a professional counselor. But if you're willing, God can turn that painful wound into a stingless scar.

Third: *Great blessings need not disqualify us.* Often, when God promotes a believer, the Christian community tends to be suspicious rather than supportive. Instead, why don't we thank God for the Josephs He's raising up in our generation? Why don't we get excited about all the ways God is going to use this believer's authority and success? Perhaps if we were more affirming and supportive, there would be fewer who succumb to temptations and fall into ruin.

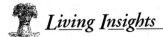
In our lesson we saw that the name Manasseh literally means "the sting is gone out of the remembrance." Joseph still carried the vivid memory of being stripped and flung into a pit by his own brothers, of being sold as a slave, of being imprisoned for his personal purity, of being forgotten for two years by someone he helped. There was enough heartache in those memories to destroy this young man, to leave him embittered, without hope, depressed, most likely suicidal.

Think about that for a moment. Was it the fancy clothes that removed the sting? The carte blanche financial clout? The chariot? No, it was God. He alone has the power to take the sting out of the hurtful past. Designer clothes may give us a momentary feeling of well-being; but underneath, the wounded memories still fester. They're still painful to the touch.

Have you ever considered asking God to remove the sting from one of your own memories? In childlike simplicity and faith, open up to Him in prayer and tell Him where it hurts. Ask Him for that same blessing He gave Joseph so that you, too, might be able to say, "The sting is gone out of the remembrance."

 *Questions for Group Discussion*

1. It has been said that the hardest test one can be put through is prosperity. Do you believe that? Why? What Scriptures can you apply to your thinking on this?

2. Joseph was seventeen years old when his brothers threw him in a pit at Dothan and thirty years old when Pharaoh pulled him out of prison to be his prime minister. Thirteen years. Does anything about that bother you? Encourage you? Confuse you about your picture of God and how the Christian life is supposed to look?

3. Many have taught and still teach that God promises prosperity— here and now—for all Christians. No dungeon days, just designer clothes and the latest model chariot. Is it wrong to have these things? Is it more spiritual to be poor? Will we be exempted from life's hardships if we are faithful?

4. Suppose you were "promoted" like Joseph was and given great

authority, title, and possessions. How do you stay humble in a position of power? What practical steps can you take to guard against the temptations that come with the title?

5. What is your attitude toward those who have more than you? Honestly, when you see someone wealthier than you and then find out that person is a Christian, are you just a little bit skeptical of that person's faith, of his or her depth as a believer? If so, why? What is that all about?

Chapter 6

ACTIVATING A SEARED CONSCIENCE

Genesis 42:1–28

ONCE UPON A TIME there lived a king and queen who wept
every day because they had no children. One day, however,
the queen received a prophecy that within a year she would have
a child. A year passed, and happily, the prophecy came true. Immediately, a great celebration was planned in honor of the favored
child. The guests included friends, relatives, and twelve kind, wise
fairies who could endow the child with magical gifts.

On the day of the great feast, however, the celebrations were
interrupted by the sudden appearance of an uninvited guest—a
thirteenth fairy, but a very sinister one. In a jealous rage over not
being invited, she cast an evil spell on the royal couple's daughter,
prophesying that on her fifteenth birthday she would prick her
finger with a spindle and die. Luckily, when the foul intruder left,
there was one fairy who had not yet bestowed her gift. Though she
could not undo the wicked decree, she could soften it. Instead of
dying, the king's daughter would fall into an enchanted sleep.

Despite this softening, the king didn't want to take any chances
with the curse, so he commanded that all the spindles in the kingdom be burned. In spite of all his efforts, though, the curse came
to pass. On her fifteenth birthday, his beautiful daughter pricked
her finger and fell asleep for a hundred years. On the very day that
the hundred years ended, a prince found his way into the castle,
wandered into the room where the beautiful princess lay sleeping,
woke her with a kiss, and they lived happily ever after.

Recognize the story? If you guessed *Sleeping Beauty*, you're right.
But this Brothers Grimm tale also closely parallels the real events
in Joseph's story.

Remember how Jacob and Rachel, Joseph's father and mother,
had lamented a long time before conceiving their firstborn, Joseph?
And how, like the princess, Joseph was also a favored child? But
because of his brothers' jealous anger, he, too, was threatened with
death. This great evil was "softened," however, by the oldest brother,
who intervened on Joseph's behalf. Instead of being cast into a deep

43

sleep at fifteen as the princess was, Joseph was cast into a pit when he was seventeen. And, as we have already seen, it was the Prince of Peace who rescued Joseph by enabling him to patiently endure his sufferings and by later promoting him to prince of Egypt.

But everything is not yet "happily ever after" in Joseph's life. In an ironic twist, the prince of Egypt is about to come to the rescue of the very brothers who rejected him. In F. B. Meyer's commentary on Joseph, the author describes what has happened to the brothers since they sold Joseph so many years ago.

> Meanwhile, the sons had become middle-aged men, with families of their own. They probably never mentioned that deed of violence to each other. *They did their best to banish the thought from their minds.* Sometimes in their dreams they may have caught a glimpse of that young face in its agony, or heard the beseechings of his anguished soul; but they sought to drown such painful memories by deep draughts of the Lethe-stream of forgetfulness. Conscience slept.[1]

For approximately twenty-five years, conscience has slept. But Joseph's brothers are about to meet the prince whom God will use to awaken their slumbering consciences and reunite a divided house.

Famine in Canaan

For the past several chapters—and years in Joseph's biography—our focus has been on his plight in Egypt. In the latter part of Genesis 41, we were told that the severe famine which struck Egypt also spread "over all the face of the earth." Now, beginning in Genesis 42, our focus suddenly shifts from the well-stocked granaries of Egypt to the empty cupboards of Canaan, from Joseph to Joseph's father and brothers.

> Now Jacob saw that there was grain in Egypt, and Jacob said to his sons, "Why are you staring at one another?" He said, "Behold, I have heard that there is grain in Egypt; go down there and buy some

---

1. F. B. Meyer, *Joseph: Beloved—Hated—Exalted* (Fort Washington, Pa.: Christian Literature Crusade, n.d.), p. 69. The "Lethe-stream" Meyer refers to is a "river in Hades whose waters cause drinkers to forget their past" (*Merriam-Webster's Collegiate Dictionary*, 10th ed., see "lethe").

for us from that place, so that we may live and not die." Then ten brothers of Joseph went down to buy grain from Egypt. But Jacob did not send Joseph's brother Benjamin with his brothers, for he said, "I am afraid that harm may befall him." So the sons of Israel came to buy grain among those who were coming, for the famine was in the land of Canaan also. (vv. 1–5)

As we follow the brothers on their journey to Egypt, remember that none of them had any idea where Joseph had ended up or whether he was even still alive. Nor did Joseph know anything about what had become of his family or that he was about to encounter his brothers in Egypt.

Encounter in Egypt

Egypt has become the soup kitchen for a starving world. Each week thousands come to buy food from the wise prime minister who has shrewdly prepared for the seven-year famine.

Dialogue with Joseph

When Jacob's sons finally reach Egypt, they stand in line to buy grain with the rest of the gaunt-faced foreigners.

Now Joseph was the ruler over the land; he was the one who sold to all the people of the land. And Joseph's brothers came and bowed down to him with their faces to the ground. When Joseph saw his brothers he recognized them, but he disguised himself to them and spoke to them harshly. And he said to them, "Where have you come from?" And they said, "From the land of Canaan, to buy food."

But Joseph had recognized his brothers, although they did not recognize him. (vv. 6–8)

To help us gain a clearer picture of this scene, let's look at some of the reasons why it may have been difficult for the brothers to recognize Joseph.

First, remember that more than twenty years have passed. The teenager the brothers had known is now a man in his forties. Joseph's voice has matured, and he speaks a foreign language as if it were his native tongue. Also, the Joseph they had known understood

Hebrew, but this individual uses an interpreter to carry on their conversation (v. 23). Hebrews also wear beards, and Joseph's face is clean-shaven in the manner of the Egyptians. Everything Joseph is wearing, from his headdress to his sandals, has an Egyptian, not Jewish, designer label. And even if the brothers do anticipate the remote possibility of seeing Joseph, it's the faces of Hebrew slaves they'll be searching, not Egyptian rulers. On top of all this, Joseph disguises his kinship even further by speaking harshly to them.

In the faces of his brothers, however, Joseph sees the visions of his youth (v. 9a). He had dreamed that his brothers' harvested sheaves bowed down before him, as well as the sun, moon, and twelve stars. Now, after all these years, his brothers are bending their knees to him, begging for grain for themselves and their families. Finally, the puzzling pieces of his youthful dreams are coming together (see 37:6–7, 9).

However, his brothers are bowing down and showing respect to the prime minister of Egypt, not to their brother Joseph. Somehow he has to find out, without revealing who he is, whether they still hate him, whether they have since felt any sorrow or guilt over what they did. One commentator said, "When the test of severe trouble is applied, and when men are thrown out of all conventional modes of thinking and speaking," that is when the true character of the heart is revealed.[2] And this is exactly the kind of test Joseph will apply to his brothers.

Plan of Joseph

> Joseph said, "You are spies; you have come to look at the undefended parts of our land." Then they said to him, "No, my lord, but your servants have come to buy food. We are all sons of one man; we are honest men, your servants are not spies." Yet he said to them, "No, but you have come to look at the undefended parts of our land!" But they said, "Your servants are twelve brothers in all, the sons of one man in the land of Canaan; and behold, the youngest is with our father today, and one is no longer alive." (42:9b–13)

---

2. Marcus Dods, as quoted by H. C. Leupold in *Exposition of Genesis* (Grand Rapids, Mich.: Baker Book House, 1942), vol. 2, p. 1048.

"No longer alive"? *But what if he is?* Joseph may be thinking. *What if he's alive and standing here in front of you? Will you rejoice and embrace him or remain bedfellows with your seared consciences?* So Joseph applies even more pressure.

> Joseph said to them, "It is as I said to you, you are spies; by this you will be tested: by the life of Pharaoh, you shall not go from this place unless your youngest brother comes here!" (vv. 14–15)

Commentator F. B. Meyer points out a fascinating parallel:

> In all this I believe *he repeated exactly the scene at the pit's mouth;* and indeed we may perhaps see what really happened there [twenty years before], reflected in the mirror of this scene. It is not unlikely that when they saw him coming towards them, in his princelike dress, they had rushed at him, accusing him of having come to spy out their corrupt behaviour, and take back an evil report to their father, as he had done before: if so, this will explain why he now suddenly accused them of being spies. No doubt the lad protested that he was no spy—that he had only come to inquire after their welfare; but they had met his protestations with rude violence in much the same way as the rough-speaking governor now treated them. . . . If this were the case—and it seems most credible—it is obvious that it was a powerful appeal to their conscience and memory, and one that could not fail to awaken both.[3]

Then, without warning, Joseph decides to imprison them all (v. 17). Why? Probably to give them time to reflect, time to awaken their consciences to the way they had sinned against their "dead" brother, and time for Joseph himself to carefully plan his next move. At the end of three days, Joseph alters his original plan. Instead of keeping all of them except one, he decides to keep one and release the others to go and bring back the youngest brother—his only full-blooded brother (vv. 18–20).

At this moment the brothers begin speaking in Hebrew, thinking that Pharaoh's prime minister cannot understand any of it. But

3. Meyer, *Joseph*, p. 72.

Joseph does understand (v. 23).

> Then they said to one another, "Truly we are guilty
> concerning our brother, because we saw the distress
> of his soul when he pleaded with us, yet we would
> not listen; therefore this distress has come upon us."
> Reuben answered them, saying, "Did I not tell you,
> 'Do not sin against the boy'; and you would not listen?
> Now comes the reckoning for his blood." (vv. 21–22)

To fully appreciate the intensity of this conversation, it's helpful
to know that the word *we* used here in the Hebrew is extremely
emphatic. "*We* are guilty"; "*we* saw the distress of his soul"; "*we*
would not listen." In his *Exposition of Genesis*, H. C. Leupold notes,

> Whatever they may have said in prison, now at
> least they speak in terms of their guilt in the matter
> of Joseph. Their conscience has awakened mightily
> during these three days. They feel that a just retri-
> bution has come upon them, and are apparently all
> of one mind in regard to the matter. They admit
> guilt, the "only acknowledgment of sin in the book
> of Genesis."[4]

One of the first signs of a conscience awakening is the admission
of personal guilt. Notice that the brothers don't blame their father
for being passive; they don't blame Joseph for being proud in his
midteen years; they simply confess their own guilt.

The brothers also talk about a *transfer of distress* (v. 21). The
distress that Joseph had felt in his soul the day they sold him has
now entered their own souls via ten fully roused consciences.

How do all these emotions and words affect Joseph? The prime
minister leaves the room so he can weep tears of relief and joy
(v. 24a). For years he has waited, hoping to be reconciled to his
brothers and be part of his family again. Now that day is dawning.

When he regains his composure, Joseph has Simeon bound[5]
(v. 24b) and orders the provisions for his other brothers' trip home
(v. 25). What his brothers don't know is that he has given them

---

4. Leupold, *Exposition of Genesis*, vol. 2, p. 1053.

5. The same eyes that once watched their brother Joseph being bound by Midianite traders
now watch in horror as the scene is replayed with another brother.

back all the money they had paid for the grain they are carrying. Once they discover the money, they turn "trembling to one another, saying, 'What is this that God has done to us?'" (v. 28). Not only have their awakened consciences led them to admit their guilt, now they're beginning to sense God's hand in their strange events.

God in Circumstances

"Once upon a time . . ." Perhaps no other four words, in any language, carry such power to awaken our slumbering imaginations for a Peter Pan flight from reality to fantasy. In this lesson, however, we have flown from fantasy to reality to help us see and remember how God used the prince of Egypt to awaken the sleeping consciences of his brothers.

Before we leave Joseph's world to reenter our own, here are two important lessons to remember. First, *God activates our seared consciences when we are victims of unfair treatment similar to what we once gave someone else.* God used the distress of being falsely accused and imprisoned to rouse the brothers' consciences, bringing to mind the distress they had caused Joseph.

Second, *God activates our seared consciences when we are recipients of undeserved expressions of grace.* His brothers deserved imprisonment or even worse for what they had done to Joseph. But what they received instead was their money back for the grain they were carrying home to Canaan. It was an act of grace from Joseph that God used to further convict his brothers and draw their attention toward Him.

🌾 *Living Insights*

For twenty-five years conscience slept. Twenty-five! But did it really "sleep"?

What did each of the brothers do when the memory of their dark deed suddenly replayed itself during a lonely shepherd's vigil or in an unguarded moment just before sleep? Consider these insightful words from C. S. Lewis.

> Every time you make a choice you are turning the central part of you, the part of you that chooses, into something a little different from what it was before. And taking your life as a whole, with all your

innumerable choices, all your life long you are slowly turning this central thing either into a heavenly creature or into a hellish creature: either into a creature that is in harmony with God, and with other creatures, and with itself, or else into one that is in a state of war and hatred with God, and with its fellow-creatures, and with itself. To be the one kind of creature is . . . joy and peace and knowledge and power. To be the other means madness, horror, idiocy, rage, impotence, and eternal loneliness. Each of us at each moment is progressing to the one state or the other.[6]

For twenty-five years, the brothers made the choice again and again to suppress the truth, to refuse repentance, to play the lie and sear their own consciences. By the time they bowed before Joseph, what kind of men were they? How do you think these choices had affected that "central" part of who they were and how they related to others?

Our choices, even the little ones that we consider inconsequential, imprint themselves on our consciences, the guardian of our souls. If you were to give a verbal snapshot of the strength or weakness of your conscience, what would it be? What choices in business, family, and other outside relationships have made it so? Would you say that the central part of you is more heavenly today than it was last year or the year before?

---

6. C. S. Lewis, Mere Christianity, rev. and enl. (New York, N.Y.: Macmillan Publishing Co., Collier Books, 1952), pp. 72–73.

 *Questions for Group Discussion*

1. Has there been a time when you were broadsided by an unexpected "test of severe trouble"? What strengths and weaknesses in your character were revealed to you in that time of stress?

2. Everyone makes mistakes, but not everyone humbly admits them and seeks forgiveness. Do you respect someone more or less when they admit their mistake?

3. What are some of the consequences of unconfessed sin (see Ps. 32:3–4)? What are the benefits of confessed sin? Have you experienced or are you experiencing anything similar right now?

4. "What goes around, comes around." Sooner or later, we all have the unpleasant experience of receiving a dose of the very mistreatment we once gave someone else. Take a moment to share what that was for you, what you learned, and how it has since affected your treatment of others facing that same situation.

5. We are so quick to judge, so slow to show compassion, so slow to give grace. If we do not recognize our need for grace, offering it to others is very hard (read and consider the relationship between love and grace in Luke 7:36–50). Can you talk about a time in your life when you received God's grace from someone or through His Word? How has that changed the way you live and relate to others?

Chapter 7

GROANINGS OF A SAD DAD

Genesis 42:29–43:15

H ave you ever accidentally dropped an open-faced peanut butter
and jelly sandwich? In that split second before impact, your
eyes widen with childlike optimism and horror. You hope you're
about to witness the miracle of the world's first peanut butter and
jelly sandwich landing right side up. But you're also horrified by
the possibilities if the sandwich belly flops. Who knows, though,
maybe this time will be different, maybe despite gravity and Mur-
phy's Law, your little sandwich will be the sandwich that could,
maybe, oh just maybe . . . *splat!* Sigh.

What's worse is when we have days where everything we do seems
to land peanut-butter-and-jelly side down. Days when there seems
to be this inexorable force thwarting and frustrating our every move.

Natural Tendencies in All of Us

All of us have days like that. And early on we develop three
reflexive responses to them—responses that are deeply rooted in
our human nature.

First, we tend to respond negatively rather than positively to
life's challenges.

Second, we tend to view problems horizontally, from a strictly human point of view, rather than from a vertical, godly perspective. Usually, it's only *after* we've made things worse by trying to solve a problem
on our own that we begin to look at things from God's perspective.

Third, we tend to resist rather than tolerate new ideas—
especially if they seem to offer something for nothing! "Nothing's
free in this world," we're told; so we condition ourselves to be
suspicious and closed toward anything unexpected that doesn't carry
a price tag in plain view.

If not dealt with, all three of these natural tendencies will grow
stronger as we grow older. Joseph's father, Jacob, could testify to
that. Even though he had known God for well over a hundred years,
Jacob's faith was constantly being undermined by his negativism,
horizontal viewpoint, and closed-mindedness.

Jacob's Initial Resistance and Reluctance

Beginning in Genesis 42:29, the narrative focus of Joseph's story transports us to Canaan at the time Jacob's ten sons are returning from buying grain in Egypt. Instead of this being a happy occasion, however, it's about to become a very bad day for Jacob.

The Return and the Report

To help you see things from Jacob's perspective, imagine you're hearing his sons' story for the first time, just as he is.

> When they came to their father Jacob in the land of Canaan, they told him all that had happened to them, saying, "The man, the lord of the land, spoke harshly with us, and took us for spies of the country. But we said to him, 'We are honest men; we are not spies. We are twelve brothers, sons of our father; one is no longer alive, and the youngest is with our father today in the land of Canaan.' The man, the lord of the land, said to us, 'By this I will know that you are honest men: leave one of your brothers with me and take grain for the famine of your households, and go. But bring your youngest brother to me that I may know that you are not spies, but honest men. I will give your brother to you, and you may trade in the land.'" (vv. 29–34)

Did you notice the two important details the sons left out about their trip? They avoided mentioning the three days they spent in prison (42:17) and said nothing about the money they discovered in one of their grain sacks on the trip home (v. 27).

We don't know exactly what Jacob was thinking while he listened to his sons' incredible tale. But remember, his entire background has been filled with deceit and manipulation, so it's deeply ingrained in his nature to think the worst. And it wasn't long before things did go from bad to worse, and Jacob's natural tendencies began to show.

Discovery and Discussion

> Now it came about as they were emptying their sacks, that behold, every man's bundle of money was in his sack; and when they and their father saw their bundles of money, they were dismayed. (v. 35)

Here they are in the midst of a desperate famine with no crops and no way to earn a living from the soil, and they find all this money. But their reaction isn't, "Praise God, He has provided!" or, "Thank the Lord for prompting that prince in Egypt to be generous toward us." Instead, it says they were "dismayed," which in Hebrew means "they were afraid."[1]

Immediately, Jacob's fear flips open the lid on his Pandora's box of natural tendencies, and his negativism, horizontal viewpoint, and resistant attitude come pouring out.

> Their father Jacob said to them, "You have bereaved me of my children: Joseph is no more, and Simeon is no more, and you would take Benjamin; all these things are against me." (v. 36)

"All these things are against me." Sounds pretty depressed, doesn't he? In all of this Jacob never once stops to think or ask what God might be doing. The oldest son, Reuben, senses that his father's mind is quickly closing and becoming resistant to letting Benjamin go, so he makes a last-ditch offer.

> Then Reuben spoke to his father, saying, "You may put my two sons to death if I do not bring him back to you; put him in my care, and I will return him to you." But Jacob said, "My son shall not go down with you; for his brother is dead, and he alone is left. If harm should befall him on the journey you are taking, then you will bring my gray hair down to Sheol in sorrow."[2] (vv. 37–38)

Reuben is too late. Jacob is emphatic and the door is shut—for a while.

Jacob's Final Acceptance

Gradually, Jacob goes through a progression of four phases in his struggle to deal with his circumstances.

---

1. This is the same word Adam used to describe his feelings toward God after he had sinned: "I heard the sound of You in the garden, and I was afraid . . . " (Gen. 3:10a).

2. Are they not *all* brothers? Is Jacob not still sowing divisive seeds of favoritism and jealousy?

Delay and Denial

> Now the famine was severe in the land. So it
> came about when they had finished eating the grain
> which they had brought from Egypt, that their father
> said to them, "Go back, buy us a little food." Judah
> spoke to him, however, saying, "The man solemnly
> warned us, 'You shall not see my face unless your
> brother is with you.' If you send our brother with
> us, we will go down and buy you food. But if you do
> not send him, we will not go down; for the man said
> to us, 'You will not see my face unless your brother
> is with you.'" (43:1–5)

Jacob eats the grain and attempts to go about business as usual
in hope that the problem will go away. But the famine persists and
it forces him, again, to face the sensitive topic of Egypt. Even when
he does address the need for food, though, he still completely ig-
nores the real problem: his sons cannot return for more grain without Benjamin. Judah's reminder, however, moves his father into a
second phase.

Blame and Deceit

> Then Israel[3] said, "Why did you treat me so badly
> by telling the man whether you still had another
> brother?" But they said, "The man questioned par-
> ticularly about us and our relatives, saying, 'Is your
> father still alive? Have you another brother?' So we
> answered his questions. Could we possibly know that
> he would say, 'Bring your brother down'?" And Judah
> said to his father Israel, "Send the lad with me and
> we will arise and go, that we may live and not die,
> we as well as you and our little ones. I myself will

---

3. Jacob was renamed Israel, meaning "God strives," after he wrestled with God (see Gen.
32:22–32). Why does the text in Genesis 43 suddenly switch from Jacob to Israel? Commentator Victor P. Hamilton believes "that 'Jacob' represents the suffering, human, feeling
side of the patriarch, while 'Israel' is used to underscore the office and the dignity of the
patriarch. While in ch. 43 we do see the hurting side of Jacob (v. 6), he emerges as the clan
head who gives directions to his sons about a second visit to Egypt, and commits their journey
to the protection of God almighty, El Shaddai. It is as 'Israel' that he thus functions in
ch. 43." *The Book of Genesis: Chapters 18–50*, The New International Commentary on the
Old Testament (Grand Rapids, Mich.: William B. Eerdmans Publishing Co., 1995), p. 541.

be surety for him; you may hold me responsible for
him. If I do not bring him back to you and set him
before you, then let me bear the blame before you
forever. For if we had not delayed, surely by now we
could have returned twice." (vv. 6–10)

Instead of dealing with the real issues, Jacob digresses into blaming his sons for all his troubles. He also clearly suggests, true to his character, that it would have been better if they had deceived the Egyptian official. Again Judah speaks, this time offering a solution to the problem, and Jacob's resolve against the inevitable begins to weaken.

Tolerance and Uncertainty

Then their father Israel said to them, "If it must
be so, then do this: take some of the best products
of the land in your bags, and carry down to the man
as a present, a little balm and a little honey, aromatic
gum and myrrh, pistachio nuts and almonds. Take
double the money in your hand, and take back in
your hand the money that was returned in the mouth
of your sacks; perhaps it was a mistake." (vv. 11–12)

Grim-faced, Jacob agrees to let Benjamin go, but not without gifts and money to assuage the suspicion of the Egyptian official. This same ploy had worked for Jacob once before when he took presents to his brother Esau, whom he had cheated (see 32:3–33:11). It's the best plan Jacob can think of to help ensure Benjamin's safety. Up till now, there are no vertical plans of hoping and trusting in the Lord, only a feeble hope in the horizontal—"perhaps it was a mistake."

Guarded Faith and Abandonment

Jacob may have forgotten to ask for God's advice, but he certainly hopes for His mercy.

"Take your brother also, and arise, return to the man;
and may God Almighty grant you compassion in the
sight of the man, so that he will release to you your
other brother and Benjamin. And as for me, if I am
bereaved of my children, I am bereaved." So the
men took this present, and they took double the
money in their hand, and Benjamin; then they arose

and went down to Egypt and stood before Joseph.
(vv. 13–15)

Finally, in this last phase, Jacob at least offers a prayer. Perfunctory though it may be, the words still show a glimmer of faith. A glimmer that is quickly obscured, however, by Jacob's stoic resignation, "If I am bereaved of my children, I am bereaved." This is not awe-inspiring faith.

But haven't we all had days where our faith lost its struggle against the undercurrents of negativism, a horizontal viewpoint, and resistance to new ideas? Let's not be too hard on Jacob just because we've seen him warts and all today. Rather, let's focus on three ways we can help ourselves learn to swim against the tide of our natural tendencies.

Practical Guidelines for All of Us

First: *Realize and admit your negative mentality.* Confession is the first part of the cure. This may sound basic, but you'd be surprised at how many Christians have never put into practice this fundamental truth. There's no skipping this elementary principle, no matter how smart you are, if you ever plan to major in a godly mentality.

Second: *Force a vertical focus until it begins to flow freely.* Our natural tendencies have a running start on all of us. From the moment we were born they have been active, growing, and maturing right alongside our physical bodies. By the time we realize these problems and decide to do something about them, we're up against formidable enemies. That's why we must force a vertical focus until it begins to flow freely.

The tendency to view life horizontally is not going to lie down and surrender just because we want it to. It has to be fought aggressively time and again with a vertical perspective. How? One way is to get into the habit of asking yourself the question, "What is God trying to say to me?"

Third: *Stay open to a new idea for at least five minutes.* Try holding off five minutes before you decide whether to accept or reject a new thought or development. Because once you've made a hasty decision, your pride will do everything it can to keep you from backing down.

None of us can escape having bad days in a fallen world. And it's not just what happens *to* us that makes life hard; our response to those problems and surprises we encounter often makes life even harder. Are your responses making your life more difficult?

Living Insights

In dealing with a change, a problem, or a discovery, awareness is often followed by a period of acceptance before we can take action. This process is sometimes referred to as the "Three A's"— Awareness, Acceptance, and Action.

Coping with a new awareness can be extremely awkward, and most of us are eager to spare ourselves the pain or discomfort. Yet, until we accept the reality with which we have been faced, we probably won't be capable of taking effective action with confidence.

Still, we may hesitate to accept an unpleasant reality because we feel that by accepting, we condone something that is intolerable. But this is not the case. . . . "Acceptance does not mean submission to a degrading situation. It means accepting the fact of a situation, then deciding what we will do about it." Acceptance can be empowering because it makes choices possible.[4]

When Jacob's sons returned, he faced a discovery, a change, and a problem. His worst nightmare became reality—another son had been taken, and worse, the person who had taken him was now demanding the only other son of his beloved Rachel. Eager to spare himself pain and discomfort, Jacob flatly refused to accept the Egyptian prince's demand. Accepting felt like condoning something that was utterly intolerable. So the aging father chose, instead, to do nothing. A poor choice that only delayed the inevitable and fostered denial. Pretty ineffective.

But before we cast the first stone at this aged man with our twenty-twenty hindsight, let's ask ourselves one question, Who of

---

4. *Courage to Change: One Day at a Time in Al-Anon II* (Virginia Beach, Va.: Al-Anon Family Group Headquarters, 1992), p. 256. This quote, though in no way an endorsement of AA or Al Anon, captures the essence of what it takes to face the various trials life throws at us.

us hasn't hesitated to face a painful problem because we equated acceptance with condoning something intolerable? Think about that for a moment. Is there a problem you're fully aware of right now but refuse to face? A problem, perhaps, that you have responded to with a negative attitude, blaming, or denial?

_____

_____

_____

_____

_____

Awareness, acceptance, and action. Remember that acceptance doesn't mean approval. It does mean, however, that you will be freed up to decide what you will do. Like seeking a vertical perspective and godly counsel to guide you in making effective, healthy choices. Are you willing to trust God and begin taking some action? What might that be?

_____

_____

_____

_____

_____

 ## Questions for Group Discussion

1. Did you notice the way Jacob spoke to his sons? Reread Genesis 42:1, 36, 38, and 43:6. What messages was he giving them?

2. How did Jacob's sons respond to his blaming? Did they attempt to rescue instead of confront? How? What more effective way could they have responded?

3. Continual caustic sarcasm, put-downs, blame—do you know what this is called? Emotional abuse. Not exactly the kind of behavior that fosters close, loving, healthy relationships. Have

you ever experienced this kind of emotional abuse? What effect did it have?

4. Think about the messages you give your family. Are your words constructive and life-giving, reflecting your faith? Or are your words harsh and cutting, withering the souls of those around you? What are you doing that you like? What would you change?

5. When all else fails, pray. "Take . . . as a present, a little balm and a little honey, aromatic gum and myrrh, pistachio nuts and almonds . . . double the money . . . your brother . . . *and may God* . . ." (Gen. 43:11–14, emphasis added). When faced with a difficult situation, which would you rather trust in: an all-powerful God or pistachio nuts? Sounds ridiculous, doesn't it? Of course. But in real life, when do most of us actually pray— before or after all else fails?

6. Denial always causes delay. What were some of the consequences of Jacob's delay, physically, spiritually, and relationally?

7. Denial can take many forms. What form did it take in Jacob's situation? What other forms have you seen? This last question is difficult, both to face and to see its answer. But try. Have respected friends pointed out any problems in your life that you're refusing to deal with, either now or in the past?

Chapter 8

FEAR DISPLACED BY GRACE

Genesis 43:15–34

A fter centuries of handling and mishandling," Frederick Buechner writes,

> most religious words have become so shopworn nobody's much interested any more. Not so with *grace*, for some reason. Mysteriously, even derivatives like *gracious* and *graceful* still have some of the bloom left.
>
> Grace is something you can never get but only be given. There's no way to earn it or deserve it or bring it about any more than you can deserve the taste of raspberries and cream or earn good looks or bring about your own birth. . . .
>
> A crucial eccentricity of the Christian faith is the assertion that people are saved by grace. There's nothing *you* have to do. There's nothing you *have* to do. There's nothing you have to *do*. . . .
>
> There's only one catch. Like any other gift, the gift of grace can be yours only if you'll reach out and take it.
>
> Maybe being able to reach out and take it is a gift too.[1]

Today's chapter in Joseph's story shows him to be even more than a man of integrity and forgiveness—he is a model of God's grace. A type and shadow of Jesus, Joseph resonates with Christ's spirit. He responds to mistreatment with blessing, and he gathers those who have long been alienated into a family.

His fearful brothers, however, haven't had the advantage of reading ahead! Every step of their trip back to Egypt has been an anxious one. But every step, from God's perspective, has been readying them to reach out and take the grace Joseph has to offer.

---

1. Frederick Buechner, *Wishful Thinking: A Theological ABC* (New York, N.Y.: Harper and Row, Publishers, 1973), pp. 33–34.

En Route from Canaan to Egypt

As we saw in our last lesson, when the grain from Egypt was depleted, Jacob relented and Benjamin was allowed to go with his brothers to buy more. Jacob's sons also took along the best products from the land of Canaan as presents, as well as double the amount of money they had found in their grain sacks (Gen. 43:15).

More importantly, however, each of them carried back to Egypt an awakened conscience. Burdened with anxiety about the intentions of the Egyptian prime minister, they wonder, *Will he release Simeon? Will he let us return? Or will he use the money we found in our sacks as an excuse to imprison us all?*

Fearful Brothers with Joseph's Butler

Our story quickly shifts from the worried and guilt-ridden brothers to the eager and excited brother, Joseph, who has been waiting for their return.

Banquet Plans

When Joseph saw Benjamin with them, he said to his house steward, "Bring the men into the house, and slay an animal and make ready; for the men are to dine with me at noon." (43:16)

The wording of this verse indicates that Joseph is primarily interested in seeing Benjamin. Why? Because Benjamin is Joseph's only full brother in the family. And perhaps because Benjamin was just a child when Joseph last saw him more than twenty years ago. Seeing his younger brother now is like seeing him for the first time all over again.

Not only is Joseph immensely overjoyed to finally see Benjamin, he is also, in that same moment, reassured that his brothers spoke the truth to him on their first trip.

Uneasy Explanation

As Shakespeare once wrote, "Suspicion always haunts the guilty mind."[2] So when Joseph's steward escorts the brothers to the prime minister's home instead of to the public grain mart, the brothers

---

2. William Shakespeare, *Third Part of King Henry VI*, in *William Shakespeare: The Complete Works* (London, England: Michael O'Mare Books, 1988), act 5, scene 6, line 2, p. 540.

immediately become suspicious.

> Now the men were afraid, because they were brought to Joseph's house; and they said, "It is because of the money that was returned in our sacks the first time that we are being brought in, that he may seek occasion against us and fall upon us, and take us for slaves with our donkeys." (v. 18)

Hounded by fear, Joseph's brothers immediately seek someone out to plead their innocence.

> So they came near to Joseph's house steward, and spoke to him at the entrance of the house, and said, "Oh, my lord, we indeed came down the first time to buy food, and it came about when we came to the lodging place, that we opened our sacks, and behold, each man's money was in the mouth of his sack, our money in full. So we have brought it back in our hand. We have also brought down other money in our hand to buy food; we do not know who put our money in our sacks." (vv. 19–22)

Calming Response

The brothers fear the worst, looking at the situation from a totally horizontal perspective . . . just like their father. Ironically, it's the Egyptian steward who speaks of their God and makes them aware of His provision.

> He said, "Be at ease, do not be afraid. Your God and the God of your father has given you treasure in your sacks; I had your money." (v. 23a)

To calm the brothers, the steward not only offers encouragement, he communicates it in Hebrew, their own language. He says, "Shalom to you," *be at ease*, and, "Elohim," *your God, the God of your father*, "has given you treasure." It's the first time anyone has suggested seeing the money they found in their sacks from a vertical perspective.

The brothers have barely finished hearing the steward's astonishing words when they are hit with a second surprise. "Then he brought Simeon out to them" (v. 23b). Now they are really confused. Here they are, standing at the entrance of the prime minister's home, whom they haven't even seen yet, and already their brother is being released to them. What can possibly happen next? Well,

> then the man brought the men into Joseph's house
> and gave them water, and they washed their feet;
> and he gave their donkeys fodder. (v. 24)

Grateful Brothers with Joseph

Can you imagine how bewildered the brothers must feel? They
have come fearing the worst and, so far, have been given only the
best. Still, they cannot imagine the prime minister being gracious
to them, so they prepare their gifts in the hope that it will appease
his anger (v. 25).

Reunion

Unbeknownst to the eleven, the brother who was rejected years
ago is about to bring his family another step closer to being reunited.

> When Joseph came home, they brought into the
> house to him the present which was in their hand
> and bowed to the ground before him. Then he asked
> them about their welfare, and said, "Is your old fa-
> ther well, of whom you spoke? Is he still alive?" They
> said, "Your servant our father is well; he is still alive."
> They bowed down in homage. (vv. 26–28)

Joseph maintains a calm exterior as he inquires about their
father. But the moment the conversation shifts to Benjamin, he
can barely contain his love and excitement.

Emotion

> As he lifted his eyes and saw his brother Benjamin,
> his mother's son, he said, "Is this your youngest
> brother, of whom you spoke to me?" And he said,
> "May God be gracious to you, my son." (v. 29)

Without even waiting for a reply, Joseph blurts out a blessing
on his younger brother. And the dam holding back Joseph's emotions cracks and quickly collapses.

> Joseph hurried out for he was deeply stirred over his
> brother, and he sought a place to weep; and he en-
> tered his chamber and wept there. (v. 30)

Later, when Joseph is finally able to control his emotions, he returns and orders the promised meal to be served (v. 31).

> So they served him by himself, and them by themselves, and the Egyptians who ate with him by themselves; because the Egyptians could not eat bread with the Hebrews, for that is loathsome to the Egyptians. Now they were seated before him, the firstborn according to his birthright and the youngest according to his youth, and the men looked at one another in astonishment. (vv. 32–33)

Commentator Henry Morris explains why they were astonished.

> After they were assigned to seats at their table, the eleven brothers noted a remarkable thing. They had been seated in order of age, from the eldest through the youngest. If this were a mere coincidence, it was indeed marvelous. One can easily show . . . that there are no less than 39,917,000 different orders in which eleven individuals could have been seated! . . . Evidently, this man knew a great deal more about their family than they had realized; or else he had some kind of supernatural power. They had no answer, and could only wonder about it.[3]

Then the food is served and another odd thing happens that the brothers cannot explain.

> He took portions to them from his own table, but Benjamin's portion was five times as much as any of theirs. So they feasted and drank freely with him. (v. 34)

In that day, everyone knew that it was socially unacceptable for an Egyptian to share a table with a Hebrew. And yet here was the prime minister of Egypt sharing the food from his privileged table with eleven of them. And to one, Benjamin, he bestows an even greater honor by giving him five times as much as the rest. Apparently, none of the brothers resent Joseph's attention to Benjamin,

---

3. Henry M. Morris, *The Genesis Record* (Grand Rapids, Mich.: Baker Book House, 1976), p. 610.

and they all relax and enjoy the meal together. One big happy family—almost.

Application and Analogy

What a picture of God's grace we have in these scenes from Joseph's life. We so often come fearing the worst from God, and then He gives us gifts. We desperately plead our case, and He speaks kindly to us—in our own language. We try to fend off His anger with our works, and He welcomes us to His Table, feeding us with the finest of wheat, the Bread of Life.

It is amazing that the One who was rejected would work so hard to get us reunited with Him. But that's His nature.

> Therefore the Lord longs to be gracious to you,
> And therefore He waits on high to have compassion
>   on you.
> For the Lord is a God of justice;
> How blessed are all those who long for Him.
> (Isa. 30:18)

Fear displaced by grace. Are you keeping your distance from God? Fearing that you'll get what you deserve? Learn from Joseph, who embodied God's grace to his brothers. Like God, Joseph was patient, giving his brothers time and opportunities to have their consciences activated. He didn't retaliate with punishment. He responded with peace and generosity. Linger over this truth. And let it lead you to the generous God of all grace.

Living Insights

> Joseph hurried out for he was deeply stirred over his brother, and he sought a place to weep; and he entered his chamber and wept there. (Gen. 43:30)

Joseph's tears are a good reminder to us that leaders do indeed have real lives and real feelings beyond our spotlight image of them.

For some Christians, though, displays of emotion—especially among leaders—are awkward and even viewed sometimes as a character flaw or weakness. Scripture, however, would contradict this perspective. Take a moment to read and record the emotional landscape of the greatest leaders in all the Bible.

Moses (Num. 11:4–15) _____

_____

_____

David (2 Sam. 18; Ps. 22:1–2) _____

_____

_____

Elijah (1 Kings 19:1–4) _____

_____

_____

Jesus (Mark 14:32–41; John 11:1–35) _____

_____

_____

Jesus wept. Moses felt intense anger. David despaired. Elijah was suicidal. Obviously, this did not disqualify them from leadership. Could it be that it somehow made them better? If so, how? If not, why not?

_____

_____

_____

_____

The truth is, for leaders and laypeople alike, hiding our emotions has nothing at all to do with strength or being a "good Christian." It has more to do with fear, the fear of being vulnerable and transparent, the fear of being rejected. "If I let others know how I really feel, they won't accept me anymore." And you know what? You may be right. Many Christians can't handle the expression of emotion and *will* reject those who won't pretend (as they do) to never be angry or sad.

Jesus was real, though; He didn't hide His emotions. Joseph was real too. And at the right time, he will reveal this side of himself to his brothers. Until then, what have you learned about emotion and yourself that could affect your leadership, whether in the home, at the office, or at church?

_____

_____

_____

_____

Questions for Group Discussion

1. God speaks to us sometimes in the most unexpected or unusual ways. A line from a movie. An anonymous gift. Even through nonbelievers like Joseph's house steward. Have you had a similar experience lately that you can share?

2. Expecting the worst, but getting the best—grace. Joseph's treatment of his brothers provides a beautiful metaphor of God's love and grace through His Son. Think about that, and see how many parallels you can find. How many can you find in your own life?

3. It's OK to express emotions. But is it really OK to be angry with God—and say it? Have you ever done this? What will happen to those who do? How does your answer reflect your view of God?

4. Waiting allows time for repentance. Many of us are so eager to crush rebellion, so ready to pounce on the slightest sign of waywardness. What if God did that too—with you? How have you experienced the truth of 2 Peter 3:9?

5. Do you have a prodigal who needs grace and time for repentance? How do you know when to wait and when to act? How would you define waiting? In your waiting, how do you keep the prodigal from controlling the situation and your emotions?

6. Has someone ever "waited" for you?

Chapter 9

"I AM JOSEPH!"
Genesis 44:1–45:15

No one who does a serious study of Joseph's life would deny that he was a great man. And yet he never accomplished any of the things we normally associate with biblical greatness. He never slew a giant. Never wrote a line of Scripture or made a sweeping prophetic prediction. Come to think of it, Joseph never even performed a single miracle. He was just your typical boy next door, who grew up in a very troubled family.

So what made Joseph great? Why does God devote so much space in Genesis to his story? One reason is Joseph's *attitude*, how he responded in faith to difficult circumstances.

His brothers, though, still haven't presented much evidence to show that they share Joseph's perspective. But that will slowly change, with a little help from Joseph and a dramatic revelation.

The Trap: Silver in the Sack

As Joseph's feast for his brothers draws to a close (43:32–34), Joseph takes his steward aside and orders him to fill the brothers' sacks with food and put each man's money back into the mouth of his sack (44:1). In Benjamin's, however, an additional item is stowed away: "Put my cup, the silver cup, in the mouth of the sack of the youngest" (v. 2a). Joseph intends to use this cup as a snare, one that will bring his brothers back to him—and also his father.

At dawn the next day, Joseph's brothers exchange thanks and happily set out for home. However, just as they get outside the city, Joseph's steward overtakes them and accuses them of stealing (vv. 3–7). Dumbfounded by the accusation, the brothers vehemently deny any wrongdoing (v. 7). In their overanxiousness to prove their innocence, though, the eleven unwittingly hand their lives over to the steward on a silver platter.

> "Behold, the money which we found in the mouth of our sacks we have brought back to you from the land of Canaan. How then could we steal silver or gold from your lord's house? With whomever of your servants it is found, let him die, and we also will be

69

my lord's slaves." (vv. 8–9)

After adjusting their promise to fit Joseph's wishes, the steward begins his preplanned inspection. The cup, of course, is eventually pulled from Benjamin's sack, and the horror-stricken brothers tear their clothes in a gesture of extreme grief. After reloading their grain, they numbly follow the steward back to the city (vv. 10–13).

According to the steward's bargain, only Benjamin has to return to Egypt. But, and note this, all the brothers return to offer what help and defense they can. Commentator Henry Morris writes,

> This decision on their part speaks volumes about the change in character that had taken place in their lives the past twenty years, and especially in the recent period associated with the famine and their experiences in Egypt.[1]

The brothers return to Joseph's house and immediately prostrate themselves before him (v. 14). The trap is sprung and the brothers are now caught in the jaws of unfair circumstances, just as Joseph had once been at his brothers' hands. With a simple question, "'What is this deed that you have done?'" Joseph judiciously probes his brothers' conscience (v. 15). Judah answers,

> "What can we say to my lord? What can we speak? And how can we justify ourselves? God has found out the iniquity of your servants." (v. 16a)

This is not a contrived confession about the cup. Rather, it's a genuine admission of guilt concerning what the brothers had done to Joseph years ago and an acknowledgment of God's justice. This divine perspective not only shows that his brothers had become sensitive to God's hand in their daily lives but also confirms that they are now fully aware and convicted by their sin toward Joseph. The hiding is over.

The Bargain: Brother for Brother

Convinced that there is no way out, Judah offers all the brothers to Joseph as slaves (v. 16b).

---

1. Henry M. Morris, *The Genesis Record* (Grand Rapids, Mich.: Baker Book House, 1976), p. 615.

But [Joseph] said, "Far be it from me to do this. The man in whose possession the cup has been found, he shall be my slave; but as for you, go up in peace to your father." (v. 17)

On the surface, Joseph is testing his brothers, seeing if they will still preserve themselves at any cost or if they will responsd with concern and compassion for Benjamin. *Will they dump Benjamin into my hands as callously as they dumped me into the hands of those foreign traders so many years ago?* At the same time, he is also testing their love for Jacob. *Are they the least bit concerned about how this will affect their father?*

What follows in verses 18 through the end of chapter 44 is an impassioned speech that is unexcelled in all the Old Testament.

> Then Judah approached him, and said, "Oh my lord, may your servant please speak a word in my lord's ears, and do not be angry with your servant; for you are equal to Pharaoh. My lord asked his servants, saying, 'Have you a father or a brother?' We said to my lord, 'We have an old father and a little child of his old age. Now his brother is dead, so he alone is left of his mother, and his father loves him.' Then you said to your servants, 'Bring him down to me that I may set my eyes on him.' But we said to my lord, 'The lad cannot leave his father, for if he should leave his father, his father would die.' You said to your servants, however, 'Unless your youngest brother comes down with you, you will not see my face again.' Thus it came about when we went up to your servant my father, we told him the words of my lord. Our father said, 'Go back, buy us a little food.' But we said, 'We cannot go down. If our youngest brother is with us, then we will go down; for we cannot see the man's face unless our youngest brother is with us.' Your servant my father said to us, 'You know that my wife bore me two sons; and the one went out from me, and I said, "Surely he is torn in pieces," and I have not seen him since. If you take this one also from me, and harm befalls him, you will bring my gray hair down to Sheol in sorrow.'" (vv. 18–29)

Twenty years ago these same brothers had broken their father's heart with a bloodstained lie they used to cloak the truth. Now, their hearts are the ones that are breaking at the thought of causing their father any more grief. Judah continues,

> "Now, therefore, when I come to your servant my father, and the lad is not with us, since his life is bound up in the lad's life, when he sees that the lad is not with us, he will die. Thus your servants will bring the gray hair of your servant our father down to Sheol in sorrow. For your servant became surety for the lad to my father, saying, 'If I do not bring him back to you, then let me bear the blame before my father forever.' Now, therefore, please let your servant remain instead of the lad a slave to my lord, and let the lad go up with his brothers. For how shall I go up to my father if the lad is not with me— for fear that I see the evil that would overtake my father?" (vv. 30–34)

These are transformed men! The godly attitude of care and compassion for others is there. They have laid their hearts bare, they're deeply committed to each other, they're sorry for their previous actions, and they're passionately concerned for their father. In addition, Joseph's heart is pierced by Judah's own integrity and willingness to sacrifice his life for Benjamin's.

The Disclosure: Identity of the Governor

Overwhelmed by the proof that these are not the same brothers who sold him into bondage years ago, that their hearts are right and repentance has done its work, Joseph finally feels that he can disclose his true identity and embrace his family.

> Then Joseph could not control himself before all those who stood by him, and he cried, "Have everyone go out from me." So there was no man with him when Joseph made himself known to his brothers. He wept so loudly that the Egyptians heard it, and the household of Pharaoh heard of it. (45:1–2)

Imagine the confusion of the brothers. First the prime minister clears the room. They probably thought in panic, *What's he going to do to us?* Then he begins sobbing uncontrollably. The scene quickly deteriorates into a strange and uncomfortable one. The brothers look at each other, their questioning eyes full of fear: *Will the Egyptians think we have harmed their prime minister?* But no one dares move or say a word to this man of great power who has frightened and confused them since the day of their first visit.

Eventually, the brothers can tell that the prime minister wants to say something. But who will understand him? He doesn't speak Hebrew, and none of the brothers know Egyptian. Yet, when the prime minister cries out, he speaks two words in Hebrew, *Aaa-nee Yo-saphe*, that all the brothers understand—but wish they didn't.

> Then Joseph said to his brothers, "I am Joseph!" (v. 3a)

Joseph immediately asks about his father, "But his brothers could not answer him, for they were dismayed at his presence" (v. 3b). Literally, they were struck speechless with terror.

So Joseph draws his brothers near to prove his identity. "I am your brother Joseph, whom you sold into Egypt" (v. 4). Outside of his brothers, no one but Joseph could have possibly known that terrible truth. Before, the brothers feared Pharaoh. Now, their hearts melt at the revelation that the prime minister is none other than Joseph, the brother they sold into slavery.

The Response: Grace to the Guilty

Now we are going to see the proof of Joseph's own greatness in his sensitivity toward God and his brothers.

First, he knows what they're thinking, how grieved and afraid they are, and he immediately tries to comfort them. "Now do not be grieved or angry with yourselves" (v. 5a). Had we been Joseph, the first thing many of us would want to talk about is how they had wronged us and how difficult and painful our life had been as a result. But not Joseph. His first concern is compassion. Where you would expect a bitter and revengeful attitude, there is only grace. How was that possible? Because of Joseph's vertical perspective.

> "For God sent me before you to preserve life. For the famine has been in the land these two years, and there are still five years in which there will be neither plowing nor harvesting. God sent me before

73

you to preserve for you a remnant in the earth, and to keep you alive by a great deliverance." (vv. 5b–7)

In addition to showing compassion to his brothers, Joseph also generously offers to share the benefits of the position God has placed him in.

"Hurry and go up to my father, and say to him, 'Thus says your son Joseph, "God has made me lord of all Egypt; come down to me, do not delay. You shall live in the land of Goshen, and you shall be near me, you and your children and your children's children and your flocks and your herds and all that you have. There I will also provide for you, for there are still five years of famine to come, and you and your household and all that you have would be impoverished."' Behold, your eyes see, and the eyes of my brother Benjamin see, that it is my mouth which is speaking to you. Now you must tell my father of all my splendor in Egypt, and all that you have seen; and you must hurry and bring my father down here." (vv. 9–13)

In a stirring scene of complete forgiveness, Joseph

fell on his brother Benjamin's neck and wept, and Benjamin wept on his neck. He kissed all his brothers and wept on them, and afterward his brothers talked with him. (vv. 14–15)

We're not told what the brothers talked about, but there can be little doubt that the centerpiece of attention must have been the grace exemplified by Joseph.

The Application: A Lesson from the Story

This part of Joseph's story shows that true greatness is revealed not in miraculous actions but in daily attitudes and responses that have been shaped according to God's perspective and compassion.

Let's explore the formation of a godly attitude in our Living Insights.

True greatness is found in our attitude, in who we are. For it is out of *who* we are that *what* we do will flow. So many of us strive to achieve that one great accomplishment, sacrificing everything, even ourselves, in the pursuit. We do, do, do, all the while starving our character and our souls.

Joseph wasn't born with a godly attitude, it was something that he, like everyone else, had to cultivate. Take a backward glance at the ways he showed it.

Genesis 45:8b: "'[God] has made me a father to Pharaoh and lord of all his household and ruler over all the land of Egypt.'"

Verse 8a: "'Now, therefore, it was not you who sent me here, but God.'"

Verse 7: "'God sent me before you to preserve for you a remnant in the earth, and to keep you alive by a great deliverance.'"

Verse 5: "'Now do not be grieved or angry with yourselves, because you sold me here, for God sent me before you to preserve life.'"

41:52: "He named the second Ephraim, 'For,' he said, 'God has made me fruitful in the land of my affliction.'"

Verse 51: "Joseph named the firstborn Manasseh, 'For,' he said, 'God has made me forget all my trouble and all my father's household.'"

Verse 16: "Joseph then answered Pharaoh, saying, 'It is not in me; God will give Pharaoh a favorable answer.'"

40:8: "Then they said to him, 'We have had a dream and there is no one to interpret it.' Then Joseph said to them, 'Do not interpretations belong to God? Tell it to me, please.'"

39:7b–9: "'Lie with me.' But he refused and said to his master's wife, '. . . How then could I do this great evil and sin against God?'"

What do you see? What do you sense? _____

_____

_____

_____

_____

What are you doing to cultivate such an attitude in yourself? Are you feeding your soul with the Word? Are you involved in a church fellowship where others know you, care for you? Are you developing a sensitivity to see God's plan and sense His hand?

_____

_____

_____

_____

_____

God calls us first and foremost to be like Himself. That is not something we can *do*, it is something we must *become*. It takes time, attention, a willing spirit to allow His Spirit to change us. Where is the priority in your life? To be or to do? One way to tell is to look at the past week in your daily planner. If you were to simply repeat that week's priorities over and over again for the next twenty years, what will you become?

_____

_____

_____

_____

_____

 *Questions for Group Discussion*

1. How do you think Joseph became so sensitive to the Lord? It's the one thing not talked about in any detail in his detailed story. You might begin by considering how we get to know anyone intimately.

2. We have all been wronged by others. Betrayed. Lied about. Manipulated. Hurt. These wounds go deep, especially when they are inflicted by a friend or a spouse. Perhaps you're in the middle of such a situation right now. What is it that you want? To be honest, we all want a little revenge. We want to defend ourselves

to everyone who will listen. We want sympathy, we want people to be "on our side." The list goes on. But you know what? None of it satisfies. None of it heals or glorifies God. What does?

3. Consider Joseph's responses of grace and compassion. What would that look like in your situation?

4. For Joseph to respond that way, something had to happen first. Do you know what that was?

5. Have you been able to do the same toward the person who wronged you? If not, talk about it. What's holding you back? What effect is it having on your spirit not to do this?

6. Judah's impassioned speech in Genesis 37:25–28 reveals many things about the man. But perhaps you will see more if you first go back and familiarize yourself with his words.

7. It was Judah's idea to sell Joseph into slavery. And now he stands before that same brother, Pharaoh's prime minister, offering to become a slave in place of Joseph's full-blooded brother, Benjamin. A lot has changed in this man since that scene at the pit (Gen 37:26–28) and now this one in the palace. What changes do you see in this man when you compare the two scenes?

Chapter 10

THE ULTIMATE
FAMILY REUNION

Genesis 45:16–46:7, 28–30

In a 1973 article titled "Home at Last!" *Newsweek* magazine won-
derfully captured the elation in the homecoming of the first few
POWs from Vietnam:

> Everything was meticulously planned. The plane
> would land, the waiting brass would snap to atten-
> tion, the men would disembark and proceed through
> an orderly reception line. But when Air Force Maj.
> Arthur Burer and four other returning POW's ar-
> rived at Andrews Air Force Base, it didn't quite work
> out that way. At the first sight of her husband, Nancy
> Burer shrieked with happiness and—with her chil-
> dren in hot pursuit—streaked across the tarmac. She
> leapt into his waiting arms, and he lifted her up in
> a bear-hug embrace and gleefully whirled her around
> and around.[1]

Few scenes in life are more emotional than a family reunited
after long years of separation. Their eyes are wet, their noses are
running, they're shouting and dancing, they're hugging, kissing,
touching one another—they're a family again.

It's this kind of emotion that underlies our study today. Previ-
ously, we saw Joseph's brothers experience an unplanned, unan-
nounced, and unexpected reunion of their own. Today, these same
brothers are going to travel back to Canaan and bring their father
to the son he hasn't seen for more than twenty years. Reunited,
they will be a family again, at last.

Plans for the Reunion

When we left Joseph and his brothers in Genesis 45:15, they
were weeping and talking together as a family. And while they

---

1. "Home at Last!" *Newsweek*, February 26, 1973, p. 16.

talked, tongues wagged along the royal Egyptian grapevine about the family reunion over at the prime minister's house.

Pharaoh's Acceptance

> Now when the news was heard in Pharaoh's house that Joseph's brothers had come, it pleased Pharaoh and his servants. Then Pharaoh said to Joseph, "Say to your brothers, 'Do this: load your beasts and go to the land of Canaan, and take your father and your households and come to me, and I will give you the best of the land of Egypt and you will eat the fat of the land.' Now you are ordered, 'Do this: take wagons from the land of Egypt for your little ones and for your wives, and bring your father and come. Do not concern yourselves with your goods, for the best of all the land of Egypt is yours.'" (vv. 16–20)

By divine providence, Pharaoh not only endorses Joseph's plan to bring his family to Egypt, he also graciously supplies the wagons that will speed the return of Joseph's aging father.

Joseph's Provisions

The wagons are quickly rounded up, and Joseph begins outfitting his brothers with provisions and presents.

> To each of them he gave changes of garments, but to Benjamin he gave three hundred pieces of silver and five changes of garments. To his father he sent as follows: ten donkeys loaded with the best things of Egypt, and ten female donkeys loaded with grain and bread and sustenance for his father on the journey. So he sent his brothers away, and as they departed, he said to them, "Do not quarrel on the journey." (vv. 22–24)

"Do not quarrel." The Hebrew term Joseph uses is *ragaz*, meaning "to be agitated or perturbed," and it often refers to the last stage before a fight breaks out. Even though his brothers have just repented and feel close to one another, Joseph knows the terrible things that sudden wealth can do to a family. He also knows the awful power of jealousy firsthand.

Jacob's Response

Fortunately, the brothers' trip to Canaan isn't marred by any squabbles over possessions. Their minds are probably too frenzied trying to figure out how they will explain Joseph to their father. In the end, blunt seems best.

> Then they went up from Egypt, and came to the land of Canaan to their father Jacob. They told him, saying, "Joseph is still alive, and indeed he is ruler over all the land of Egypt." But he was stunned, for he did not believe them. (vv. 25–26)

The Hebrew literally says, "his heart grew numb." His sons want him to exhume a hope that he had buried in his heart years ago. "Joseph, alive?" Jacob remembers the bloody coat and feels the weight of all the years of missing and mourning his precious son. "Joseph, alive? No, it's impossible!"

Jacob's sons sense that they have given their father too much information too fast. So they back up and begin again, this time carefully bringing forth every proof they can think of to support their fantastic claims.

> When they told him all the words of Joseph that he had spoken to them, and when he saw the wagons that Joseph had sent to carry him, the spirit of their father Jacob revived. (v. 27)

With the hope he had buried long ago now resurrected, Jacob catches his breath and tells his anxious sons,

> "It is enough; my son Joseph is still alive. I will go and see him before I die." (v. 28)

Journey from Canaan to Egypt

So Jacob and his family pull up their tent pegs and move. But more than that, the whole nation of Israel is on the move. To signify this, Jacob is referred to in Genesis 46:1 by his national title, Israel, instead of his personal name.

That Jacob was about to see his long-lost son doesn't change the fact that moves are tough. They're physically demanding and fraught with uncertainties and feelings of insecurity. No doubt Jacob feels a heavy responsibility about transplanting his family from their familiar roots in Canaan to the foreign soil of Egypt. His little nation is about to cross over into a fast-paced, polytheistic society that could swallow them whole.

It's encouraging to read, then, that just before Jacob leaves the borders of his own land, he stops to seek God's assurance on whether to proceed.

> So Israel set out with all that he had, and came to Beersheba, and offered sacrifices to the God of his father Isaac. God spoke to Israel in visions of the night and said, "Jacob, Jacob." And he said, "Here I am." He said, "I am God, the God of your father; do not be afraid to go down to Egypt, for I will make you a great nation there. I will go down with you to Egypt, and I will also surely bring you up again; and Joseph will close your eyes [be with you at your death]." (46:1–4)

The one thing Jacob needs to hear, God says—and more, much more.[2] He had gone to sleep afraid and unsure, but when he awakens the next morning, he is confident and eager to get underway. "God is with us; He's going to make us into a great nation; I'm going to see Joseph!"

Reunion with Joseph

Israel is only seventy strong when they enter Egypt (v. 27b)—just a tiny nation that will one day return to Canaan about two million strong. But for now they're just a small clan plodding past the stares of snooty Egyptians. They aren't even sure where they're supposed to go. So Jacob sends Judah ahead to ask Joseph for directions, and they eventually arrive at their new home in Goshen (v. 28). And it isn't long before Jacob feels the embrace of his favorite son.

> Joseph prepared his chariot and went up to Goshen to meet his father Israel; as soon as he appeared before him, he fell on his neck and wept on his neck a long time. Then Israel said to Joseph, "Now let

2. First the Lord revealed Himself to Jacob, "I am God" (v. 3a). Next, He relieved Jacob's fears, "Do not be afraid to go" (v. 3b). Then He promised to make Jacob into a great nation and assured him that He would go with them (vv. 3c–4a). And, finally, God promised to bring Jacob's ancestors out of Egypt (v. 4b)—a direct prophecy concerning the Exodus Moses would lead four hundred years later.

me die, since I have seen your face, that you are still alive." (vv. 29–30)

Reunited. A father with his son, a brother with his brothers, and wives and children and grandchildren all together at last. It must have been a wonderful family reunion.

Living Insights

The reunion of Jacob and Joseph is only one of several mentioned in Scripture, each of which foreshadows the greatest reunion of all.

> For the Lord Himself will descend from heaven with a shout, with the voice of the archangel and with the trumpet of God, and the dead in Christ will rise first. Then we who are alive and remain will be caught up together with them in the clouds to meet the Lord in the air, and so we shall always be with the Lord. (1 Thess. 4:16–17; see also Rev. 21:1–22:5)

Only the Father knows the exact day and time the festivities will begin. But you can be sure there will be plenty of food for the soul. Love, joy, peace. Platters of it.

God sent His Son, Jesus, to personally deliver an invitation with your name on it. Have you RSVP'd yet? Know how? Some say your good deeds must outweigh your bad. Others believe that you must belong to a certain denomination. Still others have elaborate rituals you must perform. But what does the Bible say? Read Acts 16:16–34; John 3:16; Romans 3:23 and 6:23; and Ephesians 2:4–9.

Believe in the Lord Jesus, and you shall be saved. That's how you reserve a seat at the banquet table in heaven for the greatest family reunion of all time. King David believed, and no doubt he looked forward to being reunited with his lost son (2 Sam. 12:15–23). Is there someone special you look forward to seeing in heaven?

If you haven't RSVP'd by faith in Jesus, it's still not too late. But be warned:

> "Then the kingdom of heaven will be comparable to ten virgins, who took their lamps and went out to meet the bridegroom. Five of them were foolish, and five were prudent. For when the foolish took their lamps, they took no oil with them, but the

prudent took oil in flasks along with their lamps. Now while the bridegroom was delaying, they all got drowsy and began to sleep. But at midnight there was a shout, 'Behold, the bridegroom! Come out to meet him.' Then all those virgins rose and trimmed their lamps. The foolish said to the prudent, 'Give us some of your oil, for our lamps are going out.' But the prudent answered, 'No, there will not be enough for us and you too; go instead to the dealers and buy some for yourselves.' And while they were going away to make the purchase, the bridegroom came, and those who were ready went in with him to the wedding feast; and the door was shut. Later the other virgins also came, saying, 'Lord, lord, open up for us.' But he answered, 'Truly I say to you, I do not know you.' Be on the alert then, for you do not know the day nor the hour." (Matt. 25:1–13)

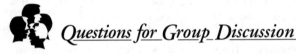 *Questions for Group Discussion*

1. "Do not quarrel," Joseph admonished his brothers (Gen. 45:24). Why? What in that present moment connected with Joseph's past to prompt him to say such a thing? If you're unsure, compare Genesis 45:21–24 with 37:3–4, 23.

2. Is it possible that Joseph repeated his father's mistake by giving Benjamin more clothes and money than the rest of his brothers?

3. Like Jacob, are you needing God's assurance concerning a "move," whether to a new location or a new job or some other important decision? How are you seeking God's guidance concerning this? How will you know when you've found it?

4. Joseph's story continues to foreshadow the Savior's. How many more parallels can you see from our study? For starters, compare Genesis 45:25–26 and Mark 16:1–11.

5. Joseph's story continues to reveal his character, but you must look closely or you'll miss the clues. Take, for example, Genesis 45:16–20. The text shows, rather than tells, us something about Joseph, even though it talks about Pharaoh. Can you figure it out? For help, read Luke 14:7–11.

Chapter 11

ON-THE-JOB INTEGRITY
Genesis 46:31–47:26

There's no reason to bring religion into it. I think
we ought to have as great a regard for religion as we
can, so as to keep it out of as many things as possible.[1]

The wit of this Irish playwright speaks more truthfully to us than
we sometimes do to ourselves. It is so easy, even practical, to
compartmentalize our lives, keeping our faith in one "sacred" area
and the other aspects of our lives in their appropriate "secular"
places. This is especially true when it comes to business.

We're told, "Business is business"—we've got to do what it takes
to turn a profit, please the boss, advance to the next rung on the
ladder. Christianity is all right on Sundays, but the Monday-
through-Friday world is a rough one, and it has rules of its own that
need to be respected if we want to succeed.

Oh really?

Is God not sovereign over all worlds, including the business
world? Since when did business take priority over character? And
when did success become more important than the relationship
with God we'll bring with us into eternity?

Joseph, as we'll see in our study, had not compartmentalized his
life into many independent, disconnected, and ultimately frag-
mented pieces. No, he lived an integrated life of faith doing everything he did in every area of life before the face of God (compare
Col. 3:17, 23). And we can do that too.

Before we learn from his example, though, let's face some important truths about our faith and business.

The Truth about Business

At least three areas of work directly affect our Christian witness.

First, *the way we work reveals our character*. It's not what we wear
or how we act for an hour or two on Sundays that demonstrates
our credibility as Christians; it's the way we behave day in, day out,

1. Sean O'Casey, *The Plough and the Stars*, act 1, as quoted in *The Columbia Dictionary of
Quotations* (New York, N. Y.: Columbus University Press, 1993). From Microsoft Bookshelf
© 1987–1994 Microsoft Corporation. All rights reserved.

forty hours a week on the job. What character traits do you display at work? Are you diligent or lazy? Truthful or dishonest? Do you gossip and sow discord, or are you loyal and enthusiastic? Would your coworkers say you're patient and cooperative or impatient and cantankerous? Do you work in a way that bears witness to the reality of Christ?

Second: *Work is a demanding arena of pressure.* In some jobs, a demanding boss or a relentless deadline builds the pressure. In others, the pressures comes from cutthroat interoffice jealousies, competition, or too much work and not enough people. In these pressure-cooker situations, what we truly believe, not just what we say we believe, is paraded in front of everyone.

Third: *Work is an exacting test of our efficiency.* Work helps us see how organized and decisive we are, how thorough, how willing to be accountable, how perceptive in spotting and correcting potential problems, and how resourceful in correcting them. It challenges us to seek God's strength and make the most of the gifts He has given us.

In the past several lessons we have focused on Joseph's relationship with his family. We have seen his divine perspective and many godly qualities. But what about the nine-to-five Joseph? What character traits does he reflect Monday through Friday? What shines in him as he comes through the refining fires of Egypt's searing famine?

A Specific Example

Let's observe Joseph's example as he handles Egypt's famine and Israel's resettlement.

> Joseph said to his brothers and to his father's household, "I will go up and tell Pharaoh, and will say to him, 'My brothers and my father's household, who were in the land of Canaan, have come to me; and the men are shepherds, for they have been keepers of livestock; and they have brought their flocks and their herds and all that they have.' When Pharaoh calls you and says, 'What is your occupation?' you shall say, 'Your servants have been keepers of livestock from our youth even until now, both we and our fathers,' that you may live in the land of Goshen; for every shepherd is loathsome to the Egyptians." (Gen. 46:31–34)

Notice, Joseph doesn't attempt to secure a place for his family by presuming upon his relationship with Pharaoh or his position as prime minister. Instead, he employs the first of several effective principles.

He Planned Ahead with Wise Objectivity

As a slave, prisoner, and now prime minister, Joseph has studied the Egyptian mind. He has learned how to live and work in a culture different from his own. And when it comes to integrating his family into this society, Joseph uses this understanding to implement some wise and objective plans. He discusses with his family his plan to report to Pharaoh (v. 31). He thinks objectively about how Jewish shepherds will be viewed by Egyptians (v. 34b). He even has his family rehearse what they will say when questioned (v. 34).

Joseph sees things realistically. He doesn't minimize the differences between his father's culture and Pharaoh's. On the contrary, his objective appraisal enables him to safely navigate his family's passage into the peaceful harbor of Goshen.

Before the family finally meets Pharaoh, however, Joseph demonstrates a second desirable trait.

He Submitted to Authority with Loyal Accountability

According to Genesis 47:1–2, Joseph updates Pharaoh on his family's arrival and introduces five of his brothers. Pharaoh discusses the brothers' future and concludes their interview by saying, "The land of Egypt is at your disposal" (v. 6). Joseph then sets up another appointment in which his father meets and blesses Pharaoh (v. 7). The outcome couldn't have been more favorable.

> Joseph settled his father and his brothers and gave them a possession in the land of Egypt, in the best of the land, in the land of Rameses, as Pharaoh had ordered. (v. 11; see also 45:16–20)

Through all of this, Joseph reflects a beautiful blend of humility and integrity. He is a skillful leader who works cooperatively with his superior. Nowhere does Joseph give the slightest hint that he resists being accountable to Pharaoh. In fact, Joseph wants Pharaoh to know what is going on. Everything is done completely aboveboard so there will be no surprises, no after-the-fact revelations, that will cause Pharaoh to doubt Joseph's loyalty.

In verse 13, the focus shifts from his family to the famine.

Now there was no food in all the land, because the famine was very severe, so that the land of Egypt and the land of Canaan languished because of the famine. Joseph gathered all the money that was found in the land of Egypt and in the land of Canaan for the grain which they bought, and Joseph brought the money into Pharaoh's house. When the money was all spent in the land of Egypt and in the land of Canaan, all the Egyptians came to Joseph and said, "Give us food, for why should we die in your presence? For our money is gone." (47:13–15)

The people are caught in a vise-like grip of starvation and desperation. Joseph has the power to tighten that grip or loosen it, since he carries the key to the granaries. It would be so easy for him to take advantage of the people. Yet he chooses to use his position to work for the welfare of others, demonstrating a third characteristic of an ethical leader.

He Arranged for Survival with Personal Integrity

Joseph brings all the money into Pharaoh's house (v. 14). He doesn't falsify any records, embezzle, or pilfer a little extra on the side for himself. He turns it all in. That's a man of absolute integrity.

Undergirding Joseph's integrity are the same two qualities he had once told Pharaoh a person in Joseph's position should possess (see Gen. 41:33). Joseph is *discerning*, perceptive of needs and how to best meet them; and he is *wise*, using his knowledge for constructive purposes. Because of this, the people are not hesitant to come to him for food when they exhaust all their money.

Then Joseph said, "Give up your livestock, and I will give you food for your livestock, since your money is gone." So they brought their livestock to Joseph, and Joseph . . . fed them with food in exchange for all their livestock that year. When that year was ended, they came to him the next year and said to him, "We will not hide from my lord that our money is all spent, and the cattle are my lord's. There is nothing left for my lord except our bodies and our lands. Why should we die before your eyes, both we and our land? Buy us and our land for food, and we and our land will be slaves to Pharaoh. So give us seed, that we may live and not die, and that the land may not be desolate." (47:16–19)

Joseph does everything he can to uphold the people's dignity. When their monetary system collapses, he opens the door for them to trade their livestock for food. Even so, it isn't long before this means of payment becomes exhausted, and Joseph's character is tested again.

The people have a plan, but will anyone listen to them? Many would not; they'd ignore the voices and ideas of those under them. But Joseph is not only open and attentive; he sees the good in their plan and combines it with his own ideas to come up with the optimal solution.

He Accepted the Challenge with Innovative Creativity

> So Joseph bought all the land of Egypt for Pharaoh, for every Egyptian sold his field, because the famine was severe upon them. Thus the land became Pharaoh's. And as for the people, he removed them to the cities from one end of Egypt's border to the other. Only the land of the priests he did not buy, for the priests had an allotment from Pharaoh, and they lived off the allotment which Pharaoh gave them. Therefore, they did not sell their land. Then Joseph said to the people, "Behold, I have today bought you and your land for Pharaoh; now, here is seed for you, and you may sow the land." (vv. 20–23)

Every challenge at work, and especially in leadership, is a call for innovative thinking. In Joseph's case, he does as the people suggest but also strategically moves them to cities for their survival. Again the people were allowed to work, thus preserving their personal dignity and national unity. Next, Joseph devises a one-fifth levy for Pharaoh and allows the people to keep the rest for their survival (v. 24). The people respond with gratitude.

> "You have saved our lives! Let us find favor in the sight of my lord, and we will be Pharaoh's slaves." (v. 25)

What started out as simply a creative idea became a successful statute that safely navigated the Egyptian empire through the turbulence of famine (v. 26).

Some Helpful Suggestions

If you were to place the private Joseph beside the prime minister Joseph, their portraits would match exactly. Joseph was not a Sunday Dr. Jekyll and Monday-through-Friday Mr. Hyde. If we're to avoid compartmentalizing our lives and live in a more integrated and holy way, we must cling to character even in the most famishing of circumstances.

Of utmost importance to every believer must be *a commitment to Christ and His standard for living.* Biblical principles, unlike business strategies, are not something to compromise. Doing so only leads to a bankrupt life.

Another priority for Christians is *the careful investment of time.* Peter Drucker writes,

> Nothing else perhaps distinguishes effective executives
> as much as their tender loving care of time. . . .
> [Without this] no amount of ability, skill, experi-
> ence, or knowledge will make an executive effective.[2]

Last, we must seek to maintain *the purest motives behind our dealings with people.* We must keep constant vigil over our hearts, asking ourselves, "Why am I saying or doing this?" "Who am I serving— my boss, myself, or God?" As the apostle Paul said again and again in his letters,

> Walk in a manner worthy of the calling with which
> you have been called. (Eph. 4:1b; see also Phil. 1:27;
> Col. 1:10; 1 Thess. 2:12)

Part of our walk is our work. So let's do it in a worthy manner, faithfully and beautifully, to honor Him.

Living Insights

In his book *Decision Making and the Will of God,* Garry Friesen devotes an entire section to the Christian's work. The thoroughness of his treatment of this subject may surprise some who think the Bible does not deal with "real life." More than that, it may challenge

---

2. As quoted by Frank Goble in *Excellence in Leadership* (Thornwood, N.Y.: Caroline House Publishers, 1972), p. 140.

some with its radical implications. We have summed it up below. Read on at your own risk.

Our work should be marked by: sincerity of heart (Eph. 6:5), enthusiasm and diligence (Eph. 6:6), reverence and devotion to Christ (Col. 3:22–24), good will (Eph. 6:7), quietness (2 Thess. 3:12), cooperation (Titus 2:9), honesty (Titus 2:10), integrity (Eph. 6:6), and gratitude (Col. 3:17).

Our goal should be: to earn our own food (2 Thess. 3:10), to provide adequately for our own family (1 Tim. 5:8), to behave properly toward outsiders (1 Thess. 4:11–12), to avoid being a burden to others (2 Thess. 3:8), to earn enough to meet our needs and to contribute toward others' needs (Eph. 4:28), to preserve God's reputation (1 Tim 6:1), and to adorn the doctrine of God so that there is no discrepancy between profession and practice (Titus 2:10).

In relationship to our employer, we should: be submissive and obedient, as unto the Lord (Eph. 6:5; Col. 3:22); be diligent in our work, with the idea that our ultimate superior is the Lord (Eph. 6:6–8); work as hard when no one is watching as we do under direct supervision (Eph. 6:6); regard our employer as worthy of all honor (1 Tim. 6:1); show respect even to those supervisors who are unreasonable (1 Pet. 2:18); and not take advantage of a Christian employer, but serve all the more out of love (1 Tim. 6:2).

In relation to our employees, we should: not abuse our workers (Eph. 6:9); treat our employees with justice and fairness (Col. 4:1); apply the Golden Rule, treating our workers as we would wish to be treated (Eph. 6:9; Luke 6:31); be fair and prompt in the payment of wages (James 5:4); and remember that we are accountable to God, the Master of all, for the treatment of our workers (Col. 4:1).[3]

What is your work marked by?

_____

_____

_____

_____

_____

3. Adapted from Garry Friesen with J. Robin Maxson, *Decision Making and the Will of God: A Biblical Alternative to the Traditional View*, A Critical Concern Book (Portland, Ore.: Multnomah Press, 1980), pp. 337–38.

Of the goals listed, which is your greatest strength? Which is your greatest weakness?

_____

_____

_____

_____

_____

In relationship to your employer, are you doing your work "heartily, as for the Lord" (Col. 3:23)? Do you show respect even to those supervisors who are unreasonable?

_____

_____

_____

_____

_____

On a one-to-ten scale, ten being best, how would you evaluate your relationships with those who work under you? _____ What could you do to improve your witness in those relationships?

_____

_____

_____

_____

_____

 *Questions for Group Discussion*

1. Joseph advised his brothers to tell Pharaoh they had been keepers of livestock since their youth (Gen. 46:33–34). Navigating sensitive cultural differences takes shrewd business sense. But when does shrewd business sense cross the line of honesty? Have

you ever been faced with something similar? Share your experience—what you struggled with, what you decided, and what you might do differently, if anything, today.

2. Of all the work-related Scripture passages Friesen lists, which reveals the area that you need the most improvement in, and why? Where do you see your greatest strength?

3. Why did Joseph not simply give the grain away to the starving people? In what ways can you apply this same principle in your relationships with your children or someone at work or someone in need?

4. Joseph had saved untold thousands of lives—indeed, Pharaoh's entire empire. Then his own family needed help. Amazingly, he did not presume upon his position, thinking, "Pharaoh owes me." He didn't march into Pharaoh's presence and make demands, nor did he try an end run behind Pharaoh's back to get what he wanted through a little manipulation. So many of us today nurse just the opposite attitude. "The government owes me." "My boss owes me." "The company owes me." "Life's not fair, so I'm going to even it up by grabbing a little for myself." A little tax money—"They'll never miss it." A little time padded on my time card—"What they don't know won't hurt them." A few office supplies for personal use—"Everybody does it." Do you find yourself thinking like this from time to time? What is the biblical antidote for such an attitude?

Chapter 12

HIGHLIGHTS OF TWILIGHT AND MIDNIGHT

Genesis 47:29–31; 50:15–21

From the pit of despair in Canaan to the pinnacle of success in Egypt, Joseph's life has been nothing short of incredible. Few lives have seen so many ups and downs, such heartaches and happy endings as his.

In this study, we will visit Joseph and his family for the last time. Seventeen years have passed since they were reunited, seventeen years of happiness, rediscovery, and restoration.

Joseph's father, Jacob, is now 147 years old (see Gen. 47:28), and he's tired. But it's a good tired. His family has not only reunited, not only survived a devastating famine, but they've turned into a growing, thriving, though still tiny, nation (v. 27). The covenant God made with his fathers is beginning to unfold, and Jacob feels a sense of urgency to ground his family in their God-given destiny.

Jacob: Sickness, Blessing, and Death

In Genesis 47:29, Jacob prepares for his approaching death—his reunion with his forefathers. Notice, he recognizes that Egypt is not the land of promise, but Canaan is.

> When the time for Israel to die drew near, he called his son Joseph and said to him, "Please, if I have found favor in your sight, place now your hand under my thigh and deal with me in kindness and faithfulness. Please do not bury me in Egypt, but when I lie down with my fathers, you shall carry me out of Egypt and bury me in their burial place." And he said, "I will do as you have said." He said, "Swear to me." So he swore to him. Then Israel bowed in worship at the head of the bed. (vv. 29–31)

In a touching exchange, Joseph gives his word to his father, and Jacob gives his son the lasting memory of a father who worshiped.

Jacob with Joseph's Sons

A little while later, Jacob's condition worsens, and Joseph is summoned. Realizing that his father won't be here much longer, he gets his sons and hurries to Jacob's side (48:1). Rallying his strength, Jacob sits up to greet Joseph; then he reiterates the sacred covenant God had made with his fathers and himself (vv. 2–4).

Unexpectedly, he adopts Joseph's sons as his own, and through them, he gives Joseph a double portion in the land of blessing. He also blesses the younger Ephraim over the older Manasseh, repeating the pattern of Abel over Cain, Isaac over Ishmael, and Jacob himself over Esau (vv. 5–22). Jacob had learned, usually the hard way, that God often works in ways we don't expect.

Jacob with His Sons

Having blessed the firstborn son of the wife he loved, Jacob now prophesies over all of his sons (chap. 49). Commentator Allen P. Ross draws out some significant truths from this scene for us.

> A fundamental principle in God's economy is that the lives and natures of the patriarchs affected their descendants. God works out the manifold destinies of His people in accordance with their moral distinctions. Genesis 49 gives a glimpse into such a program of God. This chapter includes the last of the several great sayings of destiny in Genesis—blessings, cursings, judgments, and promises. Jacob, in faith and as God's covenantal instrument, looked forward to the conquest and settlement of Israel in the land of Canaan, and then beyond to a more glorious age.
>
> God gave His people this prophecy to bear them through the dismal barrenness of their experiences and to show them that He planned all the future. For Jacob's family, the future lay beyond the bondage of Egypt in the land of promise. But the enjoyment of the blessings of that hope would depend on the participants' faithfulness. So from the solemnity of his deathbed Jacob evaluated his sons one by one, and carried his evaluation forward to the future tribes.[1]

1. Allen P. Ross, "Genesis," in *The Bible Knowledge Commentary*, Old Testament edition, ed. John F. Walvoord and Roy B. Zuck (Wheaton, Ill.: Scripture Press Publications, Victor Books, 1985), p. 98.

Joseph, notice, receives the most blessings of all (vv. 22–26).

Jacob's Death and Joseph's Mourning

With his prophecy complete, the aged patriarch instructs his sons regarding his funeral arrangements (vv. 29–32). Then he breathes his last (v. 33).

Jacob was with Joseph the first seventeen years of his son's life. And by God's grace, Joseph was able to be with his father for the last seventeen years of his. Now, however, for the second time in his life, Joseph experiences the wrenching pain of separation and loss.

> Then Joseph fell on his father's face, and wept over him and kissed him. And Joseph commanded his servants the physicians to embalm his father. So the physicians embalmed Israel. Now forty days were required for it, for such is the period required for embalming. And the Egyptians wept for him seventy days.[2] (50:1–3)

Joseph: Grief, Grace, Glory

Joseph's narrative has slowed to the mournful cadence of a funeral procession. But an uplifting time of grace still lies ahead.

Burial of His Father

With Pharaoh's permission, Joseph goes up with a great company of chariots and horsemen and even Egyptian dignitaries to the cave of Machpelah in Canaan and buries his father (50:4–14). Commentator Joyce Baldwin explains the deeper significance of this return.

> Despite the prominence of Joseph in the government of Egypt, the family would never consider its inheritance to be in Egypt. The legitimacy of their claim to Canaan lay with the divine gift of the land to Abraham, the first forefather of Israel. . . . The return of the funeral cortege from Egypt for Jacob's burial there renewed the family's claim to the cave,

---

2. In her commentary *The Message of Genesis 12–50*, Joyce Baldwin explains that "public mourning for a Pharaoh did not last longer than seventy-two days, so Jacob/Israel was greatly honoured." (Downers Grove, Ill.: InterVarsity Press, 1986), p. 215.

and also to the land. It was a pledge that they would one day return to occupy what had in fact been bestowed on Abraham and Sarah, Isaac and Rebekah. Leah too was buried there (but not Rachel), and Jacob would take his place in the family mausoleum, as one of the three great names for ever associated with God's promise of the land: Abraham, Isaac and Jacob.[3]

Forgiveness of His Brothers

In the wake of their father's death, Joseph's brothers feel something more than loss—they begin to feel the prickling stings of fear. After seventeen years, they still aren't sure of the genuineness of Joseph's love for them, and they dread his wrath.

> When Joseph's brothers saw that their father was dead, they said, "What if Joseph should bear a grudge against us and pay us back in full for all the wrong which we did to him!" So they sent a message to Joseph, saying, "Your father charged before he died, saying, 'Thus you shall say to Joseph, "Please forgive, I beg you, the transgression of your brothers and their sin, for they did you wrong."'" And now, please forgive the transgression of the servants of the God of your father." (vv. 15–17a)

According to verse 18, the brothers go so far as to throw themselves at Joseph's feet, promising to be his servants in order to win his mercy. But their unfounded and, evidently, unresolved guilt and fear only make Joseph weep (v. 17b). Gently, he assuages their anxiety with these words of forgiveness and grace.

> But Joseph said to them, "Do not be afraid, for am I in God's place? And as for you, you meant evil against me, but God meant it for good in order to bring about this present result, to preserve many people alive. So therefore, do not be afraid; I will provide for you and your little ones." So he comforted them and spoke kindly to them. (vv. 19–21)

---

3. Baldwin, *The Message of Genesis 12–50*, p. 214.

Completion of His Life

How Joseph's family and friends must have enjoyed the pleasure of his company! Instead of nursing old, bitter wounds, Joseph freely extended grace from an open hand. He led, remembered, spoke, and forgave by grace. And grace enables Joseph to enjoy his twilight years as a granddad and a great granddad (vv. 22–23). His last recorded words impart grace and encouragement to his brothers, reminding them of God's faithfulness.

> And Joseph said to his brothers, "I am about to die, but God will surely take care of you, and bring you up from this land to the land which He promised on oath to Abraham, to Isaac and to Jacob. Then Joseph made the sons of Israel swear, saying, "God will surely take care of you, and you shall carry my bones up from here." So Joseph died at the age of one hundred and ten years; and he was embalmed and placed in a coffin in Egypt. (vv. 24–26)

Today: Our Final Years

Though we've come to the end of Joseph's story, the legacy of his life lingers on. Here are just two important lessons for us to remember. First, *to grow old free of bitterness is one of the finest legacies we can leave behind.* What memory will your children have of your final years? Will it be of someone who constantly complained and never let old hurts heal? Or will it be of someone with a joyful heart like Joseph's, someone whose whole life was shaped by God's grace?

Second, *to face death right with God and others is the finest way we can enter eternity.* The grace and forgiveness that permeated Joseph's life weren't manufactured by simply looking inward, to himself. They resulted from looking outward, to God.

How is your relationship with God? How are your relationships with others? If they need redirecting, do it now. Don't wait—you could be too late. Seek peace with God through His grace (see Rom. 5:1–2, 8; 6:23; 2 Cor. 5:18–21), and ask Him to help you extend His reconciliation to others. That's something you'll never live to regret—on earth or in heaven.

Joseph left his family, his brothers, even all of Israel and Egypt, a treasured photo album of memories. Memories of a life of grace. In his book *A Father's Gift: The Legacy of Memories,* author Ken Gire asks,

> What pictures will *my* son remember
> > when he comes to the plain granite marker
> > over *his* father's grave?
> > What will my daughters remember?
> > Or my wife?
>
> I've resolved to give fewer lectures,
> > to send fewer platitudes rolling their way,
> > to give less criticism,
> > to offer fewer opinions. . . .
>
> From now on, I'll give them pictures they can
> > live by,
> > pictures that can comfort them,
> > encourage them,
> > and keep them warm
> > in my absence.
>
> Because when I'm gone, there will only be
> > silence.
> > And memories. . . .
>
> Of all
> > I could give
> > to make their lives a little fuller,
> > a little richer,
> > a little more prepared
> > for the journey ahead of them,
> > nothing compares to the gift of
> > > remembrance—
> > pictures that show they are special
> > and that they are loved.
>
> Pictures that will be there
> > when I am not.

> Pictures that have within them
> a redemption all their own.[4]

What memories of your mother or father do you hold dear? How have those images impacted your life? If you were to die tonight, what pictures—not words—would your children have of you? Would they be healing memories of grace and forgiveness, or wounds of unresolved heartaches?

 Questions for Group Discussion

1. The Hebrew custom of passing on a blessing carried with it the relational benefits of acceptance and affirmation. Are you practicing any traditions that communicate these same truths to your children? Have everyone in your group share traditions from their own families, and try to think of a few new possibilities.

2. What did the brothers' request for forgiveness reveal about them? Why is it so hard to accept forgiveness?

3. Why did his brothers' request bring about such a strong emotional response in Joseph? Have you experienced something similar?

4. "You meant evil against me, but God meant it for good" (Gen. 50:20a). Do you suppose Joseph held this belief while he was going through all of his hardships, that it was what got him through? Or did he come to this conclusion afterward, looking back? Either way, what does it reveal to you about his view of God and suffering? How does this match or conflict with your own?

4. Ken Gire, *A Father's Gift: The Legacy of Memories,* formerly titled *The Gift of Remembrance* (Grand Rapids, Mich.: Zondervan Publishing House, 1992), pp. 51, 53, 57.

BOOKS FOR
PROBING FURTHER

At the beginning of this study, we extended an invitation for you
to meet someone—Joseph. In chapter 1 we formally introduced you, and then Joseph's life story quickly took over. You were
escorted beyond the acquaintance level, past the casual "How's
work?" stage, and into the intensity and openness of intimacy.

It is our hope that you have not simply finished another Bible
study but rather gained an invaluable friend, someone whom God
can use throughout the rest of your life to tutor you in His sovereignty, grace, and forgiveness.

For those of you who want to continue mining your new relationship with Joseph or some of the issues that our study raised,
here are some books we recommend.

Bridges, Jerry. *Trusting God*. Colorado Springs, Colo.: NavPress,
1988. Based on the author's Bible study on God's sovereignty,
this book addresses our Lord's trustworthiness in times of pain.
Bridges' goal is for us to know God better and therefore be able
to trust Him more completely—even when life hurts.

Meyer, F. B. *Joseph: Beloved—Hated—Exalted*. Fort Washington,
Pa.: Christian Literature Crusade, n.d. In this book, Meyer does
a fine job of capturing the emotional nuances of Joseph's pit-
to-pinnacle story. Not only do Joseph and his family come alive
in these eloquent pages, but the scriptural account shines forth
with fresh insight as well.

The Minirth-Meier Clinic West. *Forgiveness: The Foundation of Re-
covery*. Newport Beach, Calif.: Minirth-Meier Clinic. Audio-
cassette series. This series explores the barriers we face in
experiencing forgiveness and also explains the practical steps
we can take in resolving much of our pain. For a Minirth-Meier
tape catalog and order form, write: Minirth-Meier Clinic West,
260 Newport Center Drive, Suite 430, Newport Beach, CA 92660.

Patterson, Ben. *Waiting: Finding Hope When God Seems Silent*.
Downers Grove, Ill.: InterVarsity Press, 1989. Ben Patterson
writes with compassion and forthrightness about the difficult,

sometimes agonizing, experience of waiting. Using the biblical examples of Job and Abraham, he shows us how humility and hope are the keys to enduring these painful times.

Seamands, David A. *Healing of Memories*. Wheaton, Ill.: Scripture Press Publications, Victor Books, 1985. In naming his firstborn son Manasseh, Joseph testified to God's graciousness in taking the sting out of his painful memories. In this book, Seamands shows that God's power to heal soul-scarring memories is still available.

Smalley, Gary, and John Trent. *The Blessing*. Nashville, Tenn.: Thomas Nelson Publishers, 1986. In our last lesson we caught only a glimpse of Jacob blessing his grandsons, but this was enough to show that giving a blessing was a significant and meaningful Middle Eastern custom. The life-changing power of this ancient custom is not something limited to biblical times, however. It has the power to alter the course of our lives today, and Gary Smalley and John Trent ably explain how we can successfully apply it.

Smedes, Lewis B. *Forgive and Forget: Healing the Hurts We Don't Deserve*. New York, N.Y.: Pocket Books, 1984. Smedes writes, "Forgiving seems almost unnatural. Our sense of fairness tells us people should pay for the wrong they do. But forgiving is love's power to break nature's rule." If you would like to model the kind of forgiveness Joseph was able to show his brothers, this book can teach you how.

Swindoll, Charles R. *The Grace Awakening*. Dallas, Tex.: Word Publishing, 1990. It took a supernatural empowering of God's grace for Joseph to forgive his brothers of the terrible things they did to him. If hurts from your past still haunt you, and you look on those relationships with an eye-for-eye, tooth-for-tooth type of vengeance, you need a grace awakening in your life. This book may be just the catalyst you need.

Yancey, Philip. *Disappointment with God*. Grand Rapids, Mich.: Zondervan Publishing House, 1988. As honest, human Christians who do not shrink from the truth, how can we handle those times when we are disappointed by God? Is it irreverent to feel this way, or is it merely being real? In this book, Yancey thoroughly and poignantly explores these issues.

―――. *What's So Amazing about Grace?* Grand Rapids, Mich.:

Zondervan Publishing House, 1997. In this eloquent, thought-provoking, and challenging book, Yancey asks the penetrating question, "What does the world learn about God by watching us his followers on earth?" (p. 14). Often, our lives fail to proclaim the gospel of God's grace, the heart of God's work on the world's behalf. If you would like your life to be a window to this defining trait of God's, exploring grace with Yancey would be a good place to start.

Some of the books listed may be out of print and available only through a library. For those currently available, please contact your local Christian bookstore. Books by Charles R. Swindoll may be obtained through Insight for Living, as well as some books by other authors. Just call the IFL office that serves you.

NOTES

NOTES

NOTES

NOTES

ORDERING INFORMATION

JOSEPH
A Man of Integrity and Forgiveness

If you would like to order additional study guides, purchase the cassette series that accompanies this guide, or request our product catalogs, please contact the office that serves you.

United States and International Locations:

Insight for Living
Post Office Box 69000
Anaheim, CA 92817-0900

1-800-772-8888, 24 hours a day, 7 days a week
(714) 575-5000, 8:00 A.M. to 4:30 P.M., Pacific time, Monday
  to Friday

Canada:

Insight for Living Ministries
Post Office Box 2510
Vancouver, BC, Canada V6B 3W7

1-800-663-7639, 24 hours a day, 7 days a week

Australia:

Insight for Living, Inc.
General Post Office Box 2823 EE
Melbourne, VIC 3001, Australia

(03) 9877-4277, 8:30 A.M. to 5:00 P.M., Monday to Friday

World Wide Web:
www.insight.org

Study Guide Subscription Program

Study guide subscriptions are available. Please call or write the office nearest you to find out how you can receive our study guides on a regular basis.